The Impact of the Integrated Feedback Approach

促学多元反馈机制影响研究

黄 静 著

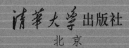

版权所有,侵权必究。举报:010-62782989,beiqinquan@tup.tsinghua.edu.cn。

图书在版编目(CIP)数据

促学多元反馈机制影响研究/黄静著 . —北京:清华大学出版社,2022.12
ISBN 978-7-302-46048-0

Ⅰ.①促… Ⅱ.①黄… Ⅲ.①英语—写作—研究
Ⅳ.① H315

中国版本图书馆 CIP 数据核字(2017)第 005023 号

| 责任编辑:徐博文　朱　琳
| 封面设计:子　一
| 责任校对:王凤芝
| 责任印制:丛怀宇

| 出版发行:清华大学出版社
| 　网　　址:http://www.tup.com.cn, http://www.wqbook.com
| 　地　　址:北京清华大学学研大厦 A 座　　邮　编:100084
| 　社 总 机:010-83470000　　　　　　　　　邮　购:010-62786544
| 　投稿与读者服务:010-62776969, c-service@tup.tsinghua.edu.cn
| 　质量反馈:010-62772015, zhiliang@tup.tsinghua.edu.cn
| 印 装 者:三河市东方印刷有限公司
| 经　　销:全国新华书店
| 开　　本:155mm×230mm　　印　张:15　　字　数:199 千字
| 版　　次:2022 年 12 月第 1 版　　印　次:2022 年 12 月第 1 次印刷
| 定　　价:118.00 元

产品编号:068589-01

Forward

Dr. Huang Jing has a rigorous academic research spirit and actively participates in various academic activities, and comprehensively understands the theory and research results of relevant research fields.

In the spring of 2012, I first met Dr. Huang Jing, who was studying for her PhD degree in the Department of Foreign Languages at Tsinghua University. At that time, she came to Renmin University of China to participate in a series of lectures given by Professor Andrew Cohen of the University of Minnesota, who is an internationally renowned scholar in the field of applied linguistics. During one-week-long lectures, Dr. Huang Jing actively discussed with Professor Cohen on the research methods and the writing of her own book, which left a very deep impression on me.

In the fall of 2012, at the International Conference on Teaching and Researching EFL Writing, Dr. Huang Jing and I met for the second time in Jinan, Shandong Province. Through these contacts, I had a comprehensive understanding of the topic and progress of her doctoral project. After that, Dr. Huang Jing contacted me on many occasions to discuss issues such as data collection, data analysis and chapter arrangement of her book. I found her basic knowledge of the discipline is solid and profound.

After Dr. Huang Jing completed her doctoral thesis in October 2013, I was invited to participate in her doctoral thesis oral defense. The main innovations of her book are as follows: 1) Her research perspective is novel. She based her research in the framework of Assessment for Learning; 2) She successfully implemented the multi-feedback mechanism in the TESOL writing course; 3) She has also organically combined written evaluation, machine automatic evaluation and oral recording evaluation in English writing course, giving full play to the advantages and functions of different subjects such as teachers, peers, students themselves, and network technology.

As one of her doctoral thesis defense committee members, I hope that Dr. Huang Jing's book can be read by a wider audience, so that its scientific research achievements can inspire on-service teachers and relevant researchers in a wider scope.

Professor, Doctoral Supervisor
School of Foreign Languages
Renmin University of China
Wu Hongyun

Preface

I have worked for 20 years as an English language lecturer at three universities in China together with one and a half years' work experience as a visiting scholar with a CSC scholarship from the Chinese government at Victoria University of Wellington in New Zealand. Within the 15 years, I have been concentrating on the teaching of Academic English Writing to undergraduate and Language Testing to MA students at the tertiary level in China. My principal duties have been the curriculum design and delivery of English writing courses at a range of levels, along with the supervision and guidance of undergraduate and MA thesis writers.

By so, I grasped the writing assessment principles and procedures of language assessment, especially classroom-based writing assessment and feedback. The book was formulated based on my long-time research and teaching experience.

How to provide effective feedback on students' writing has become one of the many research focuses worldwide for foreign language teaching practitioners and researchers. In order to overcome the limitations of the summative one-shot feedback approach, a four-stage integrated feedback approach was proposed as the result of synthesizing the related social learning theories and the Assessment for Learning (AFL) theories, as well as taking into consideration the current educational technology development and the researcher's teaching experience. This study further explored how the integrated feedback approach influenced students' perceptions and their writing performance.

In view of the research issue, a mixed-method case study research design in a longitudinal manner was employed to study twenty-five participating students how to learn to write in English in a naturalistic classroom setting over a semester rather than a short-term experimental feedback treatment. The study was conducted with a triangulation of data collection and analysis: multiple sources of data included pre- and post-course writing tests, student writing samples, reflective journals, questionnaires, interviews, and classroom observation; multiple data analysis included content analysis, frequency analysis, textual analysis, *t-test* analysis and Analysis of Variance (ANOVA).

The major findings are presented as the following: through the analysis of students' perceptions of writing learning, results show that due to more interactions, their attitudes towards writing and revising changed, they self-reported writing progress, and writing confidence was enhanced; through the analysis of students' writing performance, the participating students wrote more drafts for one task, revised more by themselves with the help of Automated Writing Evaluation (AWE) software and peer, paid more attention to language use after receiving multiple-sourced feedback, and improved the quality of their writing products to different degrees between, within and cross tasks/drafts as well as the pre-test and post-test; by investigating students' perceptions and performance, a number of factors (task-specific assessment criteria, group dynamics, etc.) were identified that may affect the implementation of the integrated feedback approach and contribute to the dynamics of classroom teaching, and assessing.

The contribution of the current research can be summarized as follows: 1) The integrated feedback approach was put forward to guide the integrated feedback practice; 2) This book originally carried out the integrated feedback practice, which contributed to the feedback literature theoretically and practically; 3) The integration of written feedback, AWE feedback and recorded oral feedback from teacher, peer and AWE software was successfully carried out; 4) This study enriched feedback research on writing in the EFL tertiary context of China.

In future research, in order to know more about individual needs and growth of the student-writers and their use of feedback from different sources, case studies of individual learners from different groups engaging with feedback over a period of time will be a topic worth exploring to provide a more complex picture of the potential of the hybrid feedback system.

Huang Jing
2022.5

Contents

Forward   I

Preface   III

Chapter 1   Introduction   1

    1.1   Assessment paradigms and feedback   2

    1.2   Dilemma in College English assessment in China   2

    1.3   Identification of the problem in feedback provision   4

    1.4   Call for research on the integrated feedback approach   4

    1.5   Organization of the book   5

Chapter 2   The Integrated Feedback Approach in Theory   7

    2.1   Feedback theories and approaches   7

        2.1.1   Feedback and teaching approaches   7

        2.1.2   Feedback purposes   9

        2.1.3   Feedback focuses   10

        2.1.4   Feedback modes   11

        2.1.5   Feedback styles   13

        2.1.6   Feedback sources   15

    2.2   Feedback in practice   17

        2.2.1   Teacher feedback   17

        2.2.2   Peer feedback   18

        2.2.3   Computer-mediated feedback   20

        2.2.4   Self-assessment as feedback   23

    2.3   Theoretical considerations   24

        2.3.1   Social learning theories   24

1. Zone of Proximal Development　25

2. Community of Practice　26

3. Meme Theory　28

2.3.2　Assessment for Learning　29

1. The concept of Assessment for Learning　30

2. The definition of formative feedback　30

3. Characteristics of good feedback practice in writing assessment　32

2.4　The integrated feedback approach: A model in practice　33

2.4.1　Stage one: The activating lecture　34

2.4.2　Stage two: The feedback process　35

2.4.3　Stage three: The feedback workshop　35

2.4.4　Stage four: The self-evaluation through reflection　36

2.5　Summary　36

Chapter 3　The Integrated Feedback Approach in Practice　39

3.1　Course introduction　39

3.1.1　Course syllabus　40

3.1.2　Course facilities　40

1. Microsoft Word Software　41

2. Tsinghua Web School　44

3. A web-based AWE program—Pigai System　45

4. Experiential Writing System　47

5. E-commentator　48

3.1.3　Course management　48

3.1.4　Course feedback procedure　50

3.2　Participants　53

3.3　Research questions　55

3.4　Instruments　55

3.4.1　Pre-course and post-course writing tests　55

3.4.2　The writing samples　56

3.4.3　Reflective journals　56

3.4.4　Questionnaire　58

    3.4.5 Interview 60

    3.4.6 Observations 60

3.5 Procedures 61

3.6 Data analysis 63

    3.6.1 Students' perceptions 63

        1. Analytical tools 63

        2. Analysis of students' perceptions 64

    3.6.2 Students' performance 65

        1. Analytical tools 65

        2. The revision performance 66

        3. The improvement of student texts 68

3.7 Summary 72

Chapter 4 Impact of the Integrated Feedback Approach on Students' Perceptions 73

4.1 Students' response to the integrated feedback approach 73

    4.1.1 Assessment criteria 75

    4.1.2 Revising process 76

    4.1.3 Interaction 78

4.2 Students' response to the feedback process 79

    4.2.1 Teacher feedback 80

    4.2.2 Peer feedback 85

    4.2.3 AWE feedback 91

4.3 Students' response to the feedback workshop 101

    4.3.1 The summary report 102

    4.3.2 The peer review presentation 103

    4.3.3 The sample pieces 104

4.4 Students' response to self-evaluation through reflection 106

4.5 Changes in students' attitude towards writing 107

4.6 Summary 110

Chapter 5 Impact of the Integrated Feedback Approach on Students' Performance   113

5.1   Impact on revision performance   113
   5.1.1   The overall revision performance   114
   5.1.2   Textual analysis of revisions   115
   5.1.3   The grammatical and functional analysis of revisions   116
      1. The size of revision   117
      2. The function of revision   118

5.2   Impact on writing improvement   121
   5.2.1   The course-related performance   121
      1. The pre-course and post-course IELTS writing tasks   121
      2. Task one and Task six   124
   5.2.2   The task-related performance   126
      1. Task A   126
      2. Task B   129
      3. Task C   131
      4. The initial drafts of Tasks A, B and C   134
      5. The final versions of Tasks A, B and C   135

5.3   Summary   137

Chapter 6 The Integrated Feedback Approach: Issues Within and Beyond   141

6.1   The integrated feedback approach: Process and product   141
   6.1.1   Students' writing process   141
   6.1.2   Students' writing product   144
   6.1.3   The coordination and collaboration of different stages   145

6.2   The integrated feedback approach: Roles of participating parties   147
   6.2.1   The instructor   148
   6.2.2   The student as peers   150
   6.2.3   The technology   154

  6.2.4 Multiple roles of the instructor and the students 157
 6.3 The integrated feedback approach: Issues and challenges 160
 6.4 Summary 163

Chapter 7 The Integrated Feedback Approach: Nurturing Positive Classroom Culture 165

 7.1 Suggestions to students 165
 7.2 Suggestions to teachers 167
 7.3 Suggestions to teacher trainers 168
 7.4 Suggestions to classroom assessment researchers 169

Appendices 171

 Appendix A: Scores of pre-course and post-course writing measures 171
 Appendix B: Scores of Tasks A, B, and C 176
 Appendix C: The assessing criteria for content and language 187
 Appendix D: The end-of-course questionnaire 189
 Appendix E: Samples of reflective journals 199

Afterwords 205

List of Abbreviations

AAL	Assessment as Learning
AFL	Assessment for Learning
AOL	Assessment of Learning
ANOVA	Analysis of Variance
AWE	Automated Writing Evaluation
CET-4	College English Test Band 4
CET-6	College English Test Band 6
COP	Community of Practice
E-feedback	Electronic Feedback
EFL	English as a Foreign Language
ERJ	End-of-course Reflective Journal
ESL	English as a Second Language
EWS	The Experiential Writing System
GC	Grammatical Changes
GRE	The Graduate Education Examination
IELTS	The International English Language Testing System
M	Mean
MC	Meaning Clarification
MD	Mean Difference
ME	Mechanics Exchange
MRJ	Mid-term Reflective Journal
MS	Mean Square
N	Number

NI	New Information
IA	Information Addition
NS	Not Sure
p	P-Value
RD	Redundancy Deletion
S	Student
SA	Strongly Agree; Structure Adjustment
SD	Strongly Disagree; Standard Deviation
Sig.	Significance
SLA	Second Language Acquisition
SE	Standard Error
TARJ	Reflective Journal for Task A (argumentative writing)
TBRJ	Reflective Journal for Task B (review writing)
TCRJ	Reflective Journal for Task C (expository writing)
TOEFL	Test of English as a Foreign Language
ZPD	Zone of Proximal Development

Chapter 1
Introduction

Since the 21st century, the world has changed into a global community. As this shift has taken place, the importance of writing in language teaching is also growing. As students enter the global community from all corners of the world, English is emerging as the international language of choice. EFL students everywhere, including college students from China, now more than ever, need to improve their writing skills in order to participate and compete in the global market. Language teaching practitioners and researchers around the world need to ask what more can be done to produce good English writers.

How can the quality of students' written work be improved? How can teaching and learning activities be designed to support students in this process? How can effective feedback schemes be utilized to facilitate students' learning of how to write in English? Over the past few decades, there has been increasing interest in strategies that focus on providing high-quality feedback to students on their work (Sadler, 1989) and in getting students to take a more active role in the management of their own learning (Butler & Winne, 1995). However, despite all these tendencies, making decisions about giving effective feedback and designing high-quality feedback practices remain a challenge to teachers in many different contexts (Hyland, 2010). The tertiary EFL learning context in China is not an exception.

1.1 Assessment paradigms and feedback

In foreign language writing classrooms, in addition to being a pedagogical tool, feedback is also a crucial device for assessment. It can be used to serve two distinct assessment purposes: formative assessment (also Assessment for Learning, AFL), which aims to assist students in the learning process, and summative assessment (also as Assessment of Learning, AOL), which is aimed at determining what students have learned. Summative assessment serves usually administrative purposes such as assigning a grade to students or placing them in suitable levels, and therefore, it seeks evidence in regards to students' level of knowledge (William, 2001). AFL, on the other hand, is usually conducted with the aim to contribute to students' learning process by providing information about their performance levels. While AOL is conclusive, and thus conducted at the end of a learning process, AFL is constructive and can take place all through the learning process (Yorke, 2003).

With a strong recognition of different feedback approaches with the two assessment paradigms, this study is to explore feedback in the framework of AFL to address the dilemma in Chinese EFL tertiary writing assessment.

1.2 Dilemma in College English assessment in China

In the long history of Chinese education, including College English learning, national examinations have often been the main drive accountable for consistent learning. For a long time, the ultimate goal of learning College English for college students in China was to pass various national tests such as the College English Test Band 4 (CET-4) and Band 6 (CET-6) or international tests such as the International English Language Testing System (IELTS), Test of English as a Foreign Language (TOEFL), and the Graduate Education Examination (GRE), rather than to acquire the ability to communicate using either spoken or written English. On the one hand, students try to determine the content of future exams through questions such as "Will we be tested on this?" or "Will this be in the examination?". On the other hand, students are commonly expected to prepare themselves for language testing and assessment by others through engaging with curriculum content. While teachers' coaching for tests has become common, this has focused mainly on the practice of similar test items rather than on helping students to conceptualize the act of assessment and feedback process for students' learning. Thus, students are effectively being excluded from a central aspect of student learning and a very important means of developing their autonomy and independence (Tara, 2001). They were subjects rather than active agents in their English learning.

In the last two decades, the College English curriculum and textbooks have made great strides in changing College English instruction to reflect many and varied goals in China. Many achievements were indeed accomplished in the College English curriculum and instruction, but complaints from the society about the low efficiency of College English learning in general and College English writing in particular didn't subdue. Is it because the assessment model that dominated in the College English classrooms limits students' English learning? A serious reflection on the question brings about the following understanding.

Assessment is the bridge that links the curriculum and drives instruction (Oleksak, 2007). The Chinese Ministry of Education has promulgated the use of formative assessment in the new version of curriculum framework of EFL teaching at the tertiary level, *the College English Curriculum Requirements* (2004; 2007), in the hope that students can improve their learning based on teachers' feedback in formative assessment and that teachers can obtain useful information from students for better instructional planning (Xu & Liu, 2009). However, until now, research on how to proceduralize the new assessment model, AFL, is quite scarce in the tertiary EFL learning context in China. Moreover, its formative potential for improving student learning in writing has been largely ignored.

Due to this situation, this book attempts to research this line of thought. It has, therefore, been designed with an aim to ascertain how AFL might be realized in a tertiary EFL writing classroom to enhance students' learning to write.

1.3 Identification of the problem in feedback provision

In Chinese College English writing classrooms, writing as a language skill has been mostly carried out in an examination-oriented manner that emphasizes summative assessment. In the writing classroom of this kind (Lo & Hyland, 2007), after assigning a writing topic, the teacher usually provides some input on grammatical structures and vocabulary needed for the writing task. Students then write within a time limit with a certain word limit, very often with the teacher in mind as the audience, and submit single drafts for teacher feedback. Thus, the feedback approach to writing is basically summative. Teachers and students are engaged in an unequal relationship, with the teachers having absolute authority over students' writing products and students only passively obeying teachers' directions and requirements for changes in their texts without knowing what kind of criteria or standards the teachers used to judge their writing. In a way, it is very hard to activate their agency through the summative one-shot feedback approach.

1.4 Call for research on the integrated feedback approach

The central concern in this research is to explore how the integrated feedback approach in the framework of AFL influences tertiary EFL writers' learning to write. Specifically, it investigates the influence of an integrated feedback approach on students' perceptions and writing performance in an attempt to locate the potential factors influencing the implementation of the integrated feedback approach. In order to achieve the above objective, the current research will focus on the following three specific purposes:

1) To investigate how the integrated feedback approach has an effect on students' writing process;
2) To examine how and to what extent the integrated feedback approach has an effect on students' writing product;
3) To identify the factors influencing the implementation of the integrated feedback approach.

By bearing in mind the previous research findings in Chapter 2, a mixed-method case study research design in a longitudinal manner was employed in a naturalistic classroom setting with a triangulation of data collection and analysis. Multiple sources of data included pre- and post-course writing tests, student writing samples, reflective journals, questionnaires, interviews, and classroom observation. Multiple data analysis included content analysis, frequency analysis, textual analysis, *t-test* analysis and ANOVA. In view of these above considerations and three research questions warrant consideration:

1) How and to what extent does the integrated feedback approach have an effect[1] on students' perceptions of learning to write in English?
2) How and to what extent does the integrated feedback approach have an effect on students' writing performance?
3) What are the factors that may influence or affect the implementation of the integrated feedback approach?

1.5 Organization of the book

Focusing on theory and practice on the integrated feedback approach, this book contains seven chapters.

Chapter 1 introduces the research briefly, including assessment paradigms and feedback, current College English assessment and major problems in feedback provision. Chapter 2 presents the related social

---

1 In this book "effect" "influence" and "impact" are used interchangeably to mean the same thing.

learning theories and the literature on AFL to connect social learning to feedback practice in the framework of AFL. Based on the theoretical discussion, the four-stage integrated feedback approach is proposed to guide the integrated feedback practice. Chapter 3 first introduces the course in which the research takes place and then the research design and methodology of the study are presented in terms of participants, research questions, instruments, data collection procedures and data analysis. Chapter 4 reports the results of the impact of the integrated feedback approach on students' perceptions of learning to write in English. Chapter 5 presents the results of the impact of the integrated feedback approach on students' writing performance. Chapter 6 draws together what has been learned based on the results of data analysis in Chapter 4 and Chapter 5 in an attempt to explore the factors influencing the implementation of the integrated feedback approach and the potential issues that were identified by the study. Chapter 7 summarizes the major findings and lists the suggestions to students, teachers, teacher trainers and classroom assessment researchers of the current study.

Chapter 2
The Integrated Feedback Approach in Theory

2.1 Feedback theories and approaches

Feedback study in writing teaching and learning can be dated back to the 1960s and the 1970s. However, feedback as the focus of writing study and pedagogy was triggered by the commencement of the "process movement" (Ferris, 2003:1). In the last two decades, feedback has become a central issue for writing research. Large numbers of articles have been devoted to considering the topic from many different perspectives, most of which have taken a pedagogical approach (Carson, 2001) and their primary focus is generally on the following areas: 1) feedback and teaching approaches; 2) feedback purposes (i.e. summative or formative); 3) feedback focuses (i.e. content, form or a combination); 4) feedback modes (i.e. written, oral or online); 5) feedback styles (i.e. questions, statements, praises, criticisms and suggestions); and 6) feedback sources (i.e. teacher, peer, self, or machine).

2.1.1 Feedback and teaching approaches

ESL writing has witnessed many theoretical changes that have led to changes in feedback. In the 1950s and 1960s, the role of writing was to help students master certain grammatical rules and to assist them in speaking performance. Tasks included fill-in-blanks, word substitution and so on, and feedback was mainly direct error correction. Those who developed the audio-lingual method of teaching (Brooks, 1960; Fries, 1945) supported direct feedback, and they believed that such feedback should be immediate.

In the 1970s the current traditional rhetoric started to take the place of the audio-lingual method. This approach provides ESL students exercises in recognizing and using topic sentences, examples and illustrations, focusing on the rhetorical patterns of academic English (Raimes, 1991). In addition to marking grammatical and semantic errors, the teacher looks for whether the students' essays follow the five-paragraph pattern, where each paragraph has a topic sentence, supporting evidence and arguments.

Some practitioners and researchers have critiqued the current traditional rhetoric of regarding writing as linear and of focusing on the written product, ignoring the process of writing. These critics have started with the process movement, which in ESL is mostly presented by the cognitive approach. These cognitivists perceive writing to be a complex problem-solving process. Hayes & Flower (1983) and Hayes (1996) describe a cognitive process theory of writing that includes planning, brainstorming, writing, revising and other processes. This shift has led to the process approach with a range of new classroom tasks characterized by the use of journals, peer collaboration, revision and attention to content before form. Feedback in this approach addresses issues like planning, organizing, and revising. Error correction comes as the final stage to improve students' writing.

In the late 1980s, the dissatisfaction of some teachers with the cognitive approach led to a shift to two approaches: the content-based teaching and English for academic purposes. In content-based instruction, an ESL course might be attached to a content course in the adjunct model, or language courses might be grouped with courses with other disciplines. The English for academic purposes approach, in which the teacher runs a theme-based class not necessarily linked to a content course, focuses on the expectations of the academic readers. With both approaches, students are supposed to get help with the language and the thinking processes, as well as the structure and shape of the content. Feedback gives students genre knowledge on how to write a good essay or research or lab report with a good introduction, a thesis statement, body paragraphs and a conclusion.

Each theory outlined above emphasizes one aspect of writing to the neglect of others. As the 21st century began, the newly theoretical trend is Eclecticism, which does not mean only doing what one likes to do; rather, it means making one's choices on a well-informed basis and adjusting one's methods to the end of engendering the optimal results one hopes for (Yang,1995). Not only eclecticism is a widely accepted theory in the field of teaching composition, evidence from writing classrooms also indicates that it is a common practice of writing teachers. Thus, to match the new philosophy of teaching writing, this study proposes and employs an integrated feedback approach by synthesizing different feedback focuses, sources, modes and styles in the framework of AFL.

2.1.2 Feedback purposes

Another argument regarding feedback is whether the purpose should be formative or summative. Summative assessment, also referred to as AOL (Lee, 2004), is often criticized as discouraging because it focuses on language errors without reference to specified learning criteria. Formative assessment, however, is usually associated with more positive aspects of assessment such as identifying students' strengths and weaknesses, helping students and teachers review the learning process, and establishing strategies accordingly (Black & William, 2003; Sebba & Maxwell, 2005).

As Hamp-Lyons (2007) states, attention in writing classes is increasingly paid to the issue of assessment rather than instruction. In their study, Connors & Lunsford (1993) analyze the feedback given to 3,000 marked writing papers and conclude that most of the feedback have a judgmental tone and are grade-driven. Teachers mostly expect students to understand the academic standards of the learning situation and to try to improve their performance based on teachers' judgments on the current achievements through feedback. Joughin (2008) criticizes this view by pointing out that academic standards are frequently not clear for students since these standards are derived from context-free theoretical perspectives. Rather than meeting the pre-specified learning and teaching standards, good feedback should be based on the specific setting by taking into account the contextual constraints such as linguistic, educational, social-economic and cultural background of the learners (Bailey & Garner, 2010; Hamp-Lyons, 2001; Joughin, 2008; Orrell, 2006).

In this study, a written response is located within the pedagogical context of AFL. The objective of the integrated feedback approach is to utilize the feedback process to achieve an enhancement of students' learning beyond that achieved through the conventional teacher-led methods. The approach presupposes the need to refocus feedback research and practice away from the notion of instructors providing one-way feedback to students in favor of dialogic exchanges in which instructors and students are jointly involved in conversations about learning (Beaumont et al., 2008).

2.1.3　Feedback focuses

Supporters of a process writing approach have been exploring how to respond to students' writing effectively. Most of them believe that teachers should respond to content in initial drafts before providing feedback on linguistic accuracy in subsequent drafts. By doing so, they support that the teacher can encourage students to make large-scale changes to content in initial drafts before helping them with small-scale changes to linguistic accuracy in the final version. It is still unclear, however, whether the content-then-form pattern of teacher response is in fact more effective than other patterns or not. However, it is believed by some practitioners and researchers that focusing on form too early in the writing process can discourage students from further polishing their texts. Others think that providing content feedback too late in the process gives no time for students to engage the feedback in-depth.

Many practitioners and researchers do believe that correcting the grammar of their students' written work will help them improve the accuracy of later writing. Although the early version of the direct opinions about teacher response in a process writing approach is expressed in Sommers (1982) and Zamel (1985), Truscott (1996) argues that teachers should give up grammatical correction because it fails to help students improve their writing by offering a persuasive case study. In response to Truscott (1996), Ferris (1999) has provided some reasons for supporting grammatical correction. These have, in turn, been refuted by Truscott (1999). Later, Truscott responded to Chandler's (2003) experimental study, which found that the accuracy of students' writing improved significantly over a semester when they corrected their errors after feedback than when they did not. Truscott (2004) questioned Chandler's findings and restated that grammatical error correction might just be ineffective, but even harmful to students' fluency and their overall writing quality.

From a pedagogical point of view, it may be possible to conclude that in deciding on whether and when to focus on form and content, teachers should pay attention to multiple aspects, such as course goals, specific task designs, learning needs and students' proficiency levels. In this study, regarding different feedback focuses, a multi-draft plus final-version scenario would be created by employing the integrated feedback approach. It follows that, if there are to be at least more stages in the feedback process, there will be multiple drafts plus a final version in the writing process. There can, of course, be multiple drafts in the writing process, in which case meaning-focused feedback and form-focused feedback can be given more than once.

2.1.4 Feedback modes

Feedback modes mainly refer to oral, written and e-feedback. In typical oral responses, writers and responders communicate and negotiate verbally and nonverbally face to face, as well as reading the text, which they can view, refer to, and mark up. It can happen in class and out of class. In written responses, responders read and then write a response on paper. Students may be required to write a response in class or by the next class. In an electronic environment, however, a L2 writer using e-feedback may not be able to participate in a series of communication activities used in traditional oral responses because the nonverbal elements are missing, or there is a time delay involved in the dialogue. Electronic response differs from traditional response in a number of areas. Table 2.1 summarizes the basic differences between oral, written and electronic responses (Tsui, 2004).

Table 2.1 General differences between oral feedback, written feedback and e-feedback

Oral feedback	Written feedback	E-feedback
Face-to-face	Face-to-face/distant	Most distant
Oral	Written	Written
Time-dependent	Depends	Time-independent
Pressure to quickly respond	Pressure to respond by next class	No pressure to quick respond
Place dependent	Depends	Place independent
Nonverbal components	No verbal components	No verbal components
More personality intrusive	Depends	More personal distant
Oral/cultural barriers	Written/cultural barriers	Written/cultural barriers
Greater sense of achievement	Greater sense of involvement	Greater sense of anonymity
Negotiation of meaning	Negotiation of meaning	Less negotiation of meaning
Less delivery effort	Greater delivery effort	Less delivery effort
N/A	No cut & paste	Cut & paste

In this study, the one-to-one teacher feedback is provided electronically to the students in the Tripartite Evaluation Model proposed by Wang & Yang (2006). The first level, "Local/Surface Corrections", is mainly addressing technical corrections to spelling, grammar, word choice, and missing words. By using the "Inter-text Notes" as the second level, the evaluator can interact with the writer through negotiating meaning, discussing, and sharing opinions. The last level is "Post-text Comments & Suggestions", where comments on the overall quality of a student's writing can be given and suggestions for further improvements can be put forward. To adapt to the research purpose of this study, the researcher added a recorded oral feedback session as part of the third level of the Tripartite Evaluation Model, which facilitates students' writing and revises processes in the integrated feedback system.

2.1.5 Feedback styles

Another main field in feedback study is feedback style. One way in which feedback style has been addressed is to include the illocutionary force of feedback (e.g., criticisms, suggestions, or comments). Researchers examining this issue have tried to determine which features best facilitate students' feedback engagement. To address this issue, Ferris (1997) examined the textual and pragmatic characteristics of one teacher's written feedback to a class of ESL university writing students. The teacher's comments were categorized according to whether they used hedges or whether they pointed out the students' problems directly. In addition, their syntactic form (question, statement, or imperative) was noted as well as their illocutionary goal (e.g., posing a question, offering praise, and asking for information). In her study, Ferris found that the teacher used comments containing few hedges and few imperatives, and most of her requests were expressed in statements. Hyland & Hyland (2001) offered a detailed text analysis of the written feedback given by two teachers to ESL students over a complete proficiency course. They considered this feedback in terms of its functions as praise, criticisms, and suggestions. Praise was the most frequently employed function in the feedback of these two teachers, but this was often used to soften criticism and suggestions rather than simply responding to good work. Many of the criticisms and suggestions were also mitigated by the use of hedging devices, question forms, and personal attribution. They explored the motivations through teacher interviews and think-aloud protocols and examined cases where students failed to understand their teachers' comments due to their indirectness. While recognizing the importance of mitigation strategies as a means of minimizing the force of criticism and enhancing effective teacher-student relationships, they also pointed out that such indirectness carried the very real potential for incomprehension and miscommunication.

When giving feedback, the evaluators should be aware of the pragmatic functions of different speech acts of the feedback. Following Holmes' (1988) characterization of compliments, they view praise as an act which attributes credit to another for some characteristics, attributes, or skills that are positively valued by the person giving feedback. It, therefore, suggests a more intense or detailed response than simple agreement. Criticism, on the other hand, is defined as "an expression of dissatisfaction or negative comments" on a text (Hyland, 2000: 44). This definition thus emphasizes commentary which finds fault in aspects of a text, and they feel the need to distinguish this from a third category, suggestion, which they regard as coming from the more positive end of a continuum. Suggestions differ from criticism in containing an explicit recommendation for remediation, a relatively clear and accomplishable action for improvement, which is sometimes referred to as "corrective criticism".

In this study, student essays are evaluated with the Tripartite Evaluation Model. It embodies three levels not only corrective feedback in form, but also content feedback from both mid-level and macro-level: Local/Surface Corrections, Inter-text Notes and Post-text Comments & Suggestions. Guidance or direction is necessary in the third level, and positive comments are generally mixed with guidance or criticism. This is in line with the advice given by Bates et al. (1993) and Hyland (2001) on how to give content feedback. Following Tunstall and Gipps (1996), feedback has been classified according to whether it is primary "person- (or ego-) referenced" or "task-referenced" in nature. The main target of "person-referenced" feedback is the student's ego. In contrast, the focus of "task-referenced" feedback is the learners' performance in relation to specific aspects of the task requirements and/or qualities and standard of performance (Tunstall & Gipps, 1996: 398). This feedback may, in turn, be classified as confirmatory, explanatory or corrective, as indicated in Table 2.2.

Table 2.2　Summary of feedback types

Feedback types		Descriptions
Person-referenced		Non-specific; affective or conative
Task-referenced	Confirmatory	Ticks; repetition of correct response; moving on without comment
	Explanatory	Highlights successful aspect of performance
	Corrective	Identifies gap between performance and expectation

Both the pragmatic aims and linguistic features of each comment of teacher feedback are executed by means of an analytical model developed based on feedback models by Tunstall & Gipps (1996), Hyland & Hyland (2001) and the Tripartite Evaluation Model as depicted in Table 2.3. Importantly, praise and criticism are taken as not only a crucial feature of the teaching context, but also as helping to constitute this context and create the interpersonal conditions in which learning might occur.

Table 2.3　An analytical model developed for feedback type

Feedback types			Tripartite Evaluation Model	Descriptions
Task-referenced	Form		Level one Level two	Vocabulary & grammar
	Content	Praise	Level two Level three	Successful aspect of performance
		Criticism	Level two Level three	Dissatisfaction & negative comments
		Suggestion	Level two Level three	Identifies gap between current performance and expected performance
Person-referenced			Level two Level three	Non-specific; affective or conative; comparison with peers

2.1.6　Feedback sources

The source of feedback is also among the debated issues in the field. While some researchers argue that the teacher is a more beneficial source of feedback for students (Carson & Nelson, 1994; Tsui & Ng, 2000; Zhang, 1995), others propose that feedback from peers provides better outcomes (e.g., Berg, 1999; Rollinson, 2005) and contributes to the development of both students who give feedback and to the ones who receive it in various ways (Lundstorm & Baker, 2009). There are other studies reporting benefits for both feedback sources. Miao et al. (2006), for example, claim that the impact of teacher feedback and that of peer feedback are different. For them, while students give much higher value to teacher feedback, they gain greater autonomy when they receive feedback from their peers. However, as the study by Tsui & Ng (2000) shows, in spite of the cumulative overall results, there are individual variations among students regarding the feedback source they prefer depending on factors such as students' culture or the quality of feedback. Therefore, many studies suggest that peer feedback or self-assessment as feedback can be assisting adjuncts to teacher feedback instead of using either as a single source of feedback.

Moving from these discussions, it is clear that there is no consensus on the nature, the content, the purpose, or the source of feedback. In addition to not providing clear answers in terms of ambiguities in giving and receiving feedback, the importance of the student factors in the second part of the process is almost totally ignored in most of the discussions. Although students are viewed as passive components of the feedback process on most occasions, there are a good number of studies suggesting that students are eager to experiment with different feedback options and to gain opportunities to voice their needs (Lee, 2007). William (2001), for instance, maintains that students are willing to play an active role in managing their own learning. Thus, any decision in the process of receiving and giving feedback should be based on the learning context and should take students' agency into consideration.

This section has provided a very valuable overview of a number of important issues related to the different areas of research currently being carried out in feedback on writing. However, despite all these developments, making decisions about giving feedback and designing effective feedback systems remains a challenge to teachers in many different contexts, and a number of questions about giving effective feedback have been only partially resolved.

2.2 Feedback in practice

Developments in writing pedagogy have been informed by feedback practice research on writing and in turn technological advances have also resulted in far-reaching changes to feedback practices. With a greater emphasis on peer and collaborative feedback, and the growing importance of computer-mediated feedback (Hyland, 2010), written feedback practices including teacher feedback, peer feedback, computer-based feedback and self-assessment as feedback are reviewed in this section.

2.2.1 Teacher feedback

Providing written feedback to students is one of the EFL writing teachers' most important tasks, offering the kind of individualized attention that is otherwise rarely possible under normal classroom conditions (Hyland & Hyland, 2001). However, generally acknowledged as pedagogically useful (Cohen & Cavalcanti, 1990; Hedgcock & Lefkowitz, 1994), the role of teacher written feedback has largely been seen as informational, a means of channeling reactions and advice to facilitate improvements. Because of this, its important interpersonal aspects, the part it plays in expressing a teacher's stance and beliefs about writing, and in negotiating a relationship with learners are often overlooked. In fact, they may be fulfilling several different and possibly conflicting roles as they give feedback: sometimes acting as a teacher, proofreader, facilitator, gatekeeper, evaluator, and reader at the same time (Leki, 1990; Reid, 1994). In addition, an instructor's personal knowledge of the writer is usually greater and he or she has more interest in creating and maintaining a good face-to-face relationship with the feedback receiver.

All of the teacher response research, for the most part, has been approached with a focus on how teachers should give feedback and whether certain feedback strategies are effective, as well as the impact of teacher response on student revision and writing (Hyland & Hyland, 2006). Little has been done to find out the role of teacher feedback plays in the larger context of teaching and learning of writing (Ferris, 2003), and specifically the functions of teacher feedback as part of an integrated feedback approach from AFL perspective. Teacher feedback in this book as part of a hybrid feedback system is trying to balance both form and content, with more emphasis on content.

2.2.2　Peer feedback

Liu & Hansen (2002) presented strong justification for the use of peer response from four theoretical stances: process writing, Vygotskian learning theory, interactionist theories of ESL acquisition, and collaborative learning. It is seen as an important support for the drafting and redrafting of process approaches to writing (Mittan, 1989; Zamel, 1985). Vygotskian approaches also stress the importance of social interaction with peers, as Vygotsky's (1978) theoretical construct of the Zone of Proximal Development (ZPD) suggests that writing skills can emerge with the help of others. While not directly driving interest in peer feedback, interactionist perspectives offer an important theoretical foundation for it by suggesting how opportunities to negotiate meaning through group work are a means of encouraging more effective acquisition of the language (Long & Porter, 1985). Effective peer response is a key element of helping novice writers to understand how readers see their work. Interactional modifications can assist acquisition by making input available and comprehensible while providing learners with important opportunities for practice, for testing hypotheses about language use against peers' responses, and for revision and writing in response to peer feedback. Collaborative learning theory (Bruffee, 1984) encourages students to "pool" their resources so that both students complete tasks they could not do on their own, learning through dialogue and interaction with their peers (Hirvela, 1999). It is therefore not surprising that peer response remains a popular source of feedback in the ESL classroom and a continuing area for research.

The research literature claims many positive effects of peer feedback in both L1 and L2 contexts. Specifically, it is seen as a way of giving more control and autonomy to students since it activates their agency in the feedback process rather than a passive dependence on teacher feedback (Mendoca & Johnson, 1994). Since student reviewers understand that their peer students commit the same difficulties in writing as they do, peer feedback may also help to decrease their writing anxiety and help enhance their confidence as writers (Chaudron, 1984; Coterall & Cohen, 2003; Curtis, 2001). Caulk (1994), Freedman & Sperling (1985) and Mittan (1989) supported that peer feedback could offer students an authentic audience for their writing instead of a teacher. Cheng & Warren (1996) and Stoddard & MacArthur (1993) believed that peer response could improve the self-evaluative ability of peer reviewers.

Studies have investigated L2 students' ability to offer effective feedback to each other and questioned the extent to which students are prepared to use their peers' feedback in their revising process. Connor & Asenavage (1994) stated that only 5% of revision could be directly related to peer feedback. Mendoca & Johnson (1994), in addition, suggested that learners were doubtful about using peer feedback in their revisions. Two explanations are provided to account for this failure to address peer feedback. First, there is unsureness about the quality of peer feedback. Some researchers (Hyland, 2000; Leki, 1990; Lockhart & Ng, 1993; Mendoca & Johnson 1994; Nelson & Murphy, 1992, 1993) have found that students have problems tracing errors and offering effective feedback, or they may give wrong or harsh feedback (Amores, 1997) or focus too much on grammatical errors (McGroarty & Zhu, 1997). Second, learners' belief in the authority of teacher and peer feedback may affect their engagement of feedback. In Zhang's (1995) study of 81 first-year university students, 75% preferred teacher feedback to other sources. Students took their teachers as a "figure of authority that guaranteed quality" in Tsui & Ng (2000: 149) rather than their peers, believing that the teacher is having more expertise whereas their peers might not be authoritative enough to diagnose their problems (Sengupta, 1998). Nelson & Carson's (1998) interviews with L2 tertiary learners found that they used more teacher feedback than peer feedback in their revisions.

However, despite these issues, peer feedback is still popular. Many teachers and course designers continue to incorporate it in their courses and to report positive experiences from students. Liu (1997), for instance, found students to be more positive about peer response after a semester's experience of such sessions. Students had reservations about trusting their peers' comments and about their peers' ability to comment on subject areas they did not specialize in, but felt they had benefited from peer response at the textual, cognitive and communicative level. It has been suggested that part of the reason for some of the negative findings may be related to the framing of research questions.

2.2.3 Computer-mediated feedback

A growing impact on feedback practices comes from the development of sophisticated software capable of scanning student texts and generating immediate evaluative comments on them. Such applications known as Automated Writing Evaluation (AWE) may assist teachers to manage the burdens imposed by growing class sizes and increasing expectations for individualized support. Different types of feedback are offered by such programs, ranging from individual reports on grammatical errors, targeting ESL students (Liou, 1994; Warden & Chen 1995), to holistic assessments of content, organization, and mechanics (Burston, 2001). Bull & McKenna (2004) argue that the use of computers in assessing written responses is pedagogically desirable as it can be integrated with existing assessment methods and strategies, increase the frequency of feedback, and broaden the range of assessed skills. Coniam (2009) summarizes the major arguments in the literature (Chapelle & Douglas, 2006; Dilki, 2006; Hughes, 2003) for using computers in assessing students' written work as money, time, objectivity, and reliability levels matching those attained by multiple human raters.

Such programs are relatively new and their impact on the development of ESL writing has yet to be systematically evaluated. Generally, automated response programs have been criticized for being unreliable (Krishnamurthy, 2005) and achieving poor pedagogic principles (Chapelle, 2001), so whether the statistical techniques they use can provide useful feedback on ESL writing is an open question (Hearst, 2000). We might also wonder whether such automated feedback systems will ever be able to deal with more than a few, very narrow and questionably useful genres. In fact, many developers of automated feedback software insist that computer-generated feedback should only be considered a supplement to, rather than a substitute for, classroom instruction (Burstein & Marcu, 2003; Burstein et al., 2004). In particular, there is little research on the social, cognitive and communicative dimensions of automated feedback or on the potential dangers of ignoring meaning negotiation in real-world contexts or the effects of isolated learning. Perhaps more seriously, while they go beyond the often misleading and prescriptive information provided by early grammatical checkers, these programs tend to treat writing as mastery of a set of sub-skills, laying particular emphasis on grammatical correctness. In the automated context, writing is not evaluated as real interaction designed to achieve different communicative purposes with different audiences but as a performance artifact of student mastery of grammar, usage, and organization. So while it remains unclear what specific advantages these new products will offer, the dangers of such systems emphasize formulaic writing which better lends itself to systematic codification cannot be over-estimated (Ware & Warshauer, 2006).

However, the research into the use of AWE applications paints a confusing picture, with some reporting positive results (Coniam, 2009; Hutchison, 2007) while others report negative or mixed results (Lai, 2010; Lee et al., 2009; Tuzi, 2004), with factors such as individual writing ability, the pedagogy adopted and the particular AWE application influencing the results (Lee et al., 2009). Previous studies on AWE for formative learning demonstrate that automated feedback is not used sufficiently during students' revising process. It is reported that such feedback is predetermined and thus formulaic and unable to provide context-sensitive responses especially to the dimension of meaning. The automated feedback is useful only for the revision of formal aspects of writing such as grammar, usage and organization but not for content development (Yang, 2004; Yeh & Yu, 2004). At the same time, studies also suggest that AWE use might be positively correlated with text quality or second language proficiency (Grant & Ginther, 2000; Jarvis et al., 2003; Yang, 2004). It is revealed that more advanced learners tend to show less favorable reactions toward AWE feedback and negative effects were also found by novice writers (Brock, 1990; Pennington & Brock, 1990). Studies by Pennington & Brock (1990) suggested that when EFL students used a text analyzer without teacher feedback, the results were that writers tended to accept the analyzer's suggestions, even when those alternatives were inappropriate. In addition, it also suggested that using AWE as an aid to provide formative feedback has more potential in developing EFL learners' writing competence and has a different impact on them in the classroom as compared with that in the first language context. According to Brock (1990), L2 writing errors are more idiosyncratic and harder to classify than L1 errors.

  AWE developers claim that these programs can be used for both summative and formative purposes. They facilitate the writing process by not only generating immediate automated scores but also giving diagnostic feedback on dimensions including grammar, vocabulary, organization and content. At the same time, AWE programs also provide a variety of writing resources for both instructors and students such as thesauri and class management tools. In fact, many developers of automated feedback software insist that computer-generated feedback should only be considered a supplement to, rather than a substitute for, classroom instruction (Burstein & Marcu, 2003; Burstein et al., 2004). AWE programs used in the classroom for instructional purposes are suggested as a supplement to, rather than as a replacement of, writing instructors (Shermis & Burstein, 2003; Ware, 2005; Warschauer & Ware, 2006). However, a further empirical investigation might help explore how AWE programs can be used most effectively in various learning contexts and with diverse pedagogical practices as well as learners' perceptions of the use of AWE in developing writing skills and motivating autonomous learning. In this study, it is used as a part of a hybrid feedback system before the use of peer and teacher feedback.

2.2.4 Self-assessment as feedback

Students can make their own revisions without external feedback and improve their writing significantly. It is therefore important not to overlook the writers themselves as critical readers and reviewers of their own texts (Hyland & Hyland, 2006). Educational research also suggests that feedback is more effective when information is gathered from the subjects themselves as well as others (Brinko, 1993). In fact, most writing teachers would acknowledge that the final goal of any form of feedback should be to move students to a more independent role where they can critically evaluate their own writing and intervene to change their own processes and products where necessary.

To do this, students need to develop metacognitive skills. Beach & Eaton (1984) have suggested a link between a lack of substantive revision and a lack of the skills to critically assess one's own work in first language contexts. Researchers in L1 contexts argued that this might be partially the result of age and level of development, but there might also be a need for specific training or instruction in self-assessment techniques, for example, Bereiter & Scardamalia's (1987) use of procedural facilitation techniques and cueing for the development of revision strategies. A problem with self-evaluation for many writers is the difficulty of reading one's own text with the critical detachment of an outside reader. It has been claimed that instruction can assist the development of this critical detachment and is therefore a valuable, if indirect, source of feedback.

It has, however, been pointed out that strategy instruction or prompt techniques to encourage self-assessment are often quite mechanical and may fail to take account of students' own goals and the context in which they are working. Peck (1990) examined the effects of prompts on revisions to an interpretative essay, using a broad-ranging and open-ended prompt. He found that writers' revising behavior varied not just because of differences in knowledge about revising and in writing competence, but because individual writers brought their own goals to the writing process and represented the task in different ways. Cumming & So (1996) compared tutoring sessions for ESL students on their writing using conventional error correction and procedural facilitation prompts and found that in both cases the teachers and students focused primarily on local errors. It seems that strategy instruction techniques are limited in their ability to improve students' revising skills due to their tendency to reduce complex processes to a simplistic formula. Perhaps more promising for self-evaluation, and discussed in the next section below, are computer-assisted packages and prompts which the students can use as a resource for checking their own writing.

There are also promising developments in self-evaluation, reflection via portfolio writing and other reflective course designs. For example, Johns (2006) described a project she used successfully: the I-Search Paper, which required extensive student reflection after the completion of a research writing task. The I-Search was originally designed by Mecrorie (1980) to encourage student reflection and develop writer autonomy and give students many opportunities to reflect upon their research and writing processes. From her experiences using this project with mainly L2 students, Johns (2006) argued her students were able to develop motivation, confidence, self-reflection, and meta-awareness skills, which thus encouraged writer autonomy.

2.3 Theoretical considerations

The theoretical conditions are mainly related social learning theories—Zone of Proximal Development, Community of Practice, and Meme Theory. Then, the concept of AFL, the definition of formative feedback and characteristics of good formative feedback practice are also meaningful to connect social learning to feedback practice in the framework of AFL.

2.3.1 Social learning theories

The influence of social learning theories of language development has focused attention on the interactive and collaborative aspects of feedback and its crucial dialogic role in scaffolding learning (Hyland, 2010). Thus, this study presupposes that the effectiveness of feedback depends on the learning theory mainly adhered to social learning theories, such as Zone of Proximal Development, Community of Practice, and Meme Theory.

1. Zone of Proximal Development

Zone of Proximal Development (hereafter as ZPD) is a notion developed by Vygotsky (1896, 1934), the famous psychologist and social constructivist of the former Soviet Union. The basic argument of his theoretical model is that social interaction is of upmost importance in the process of cognition maturation.

Vygotsky emphasized that "Every function in the child's cultural development appears twice: first, on the social level, and later, on the individual level; second, between people and then inside the child" (1978: 57). Another part of Vygotsky's theory is the idea that the potential for cognitive development depends upon the ZPD in Figure 2.1. The reach of skill that can be achieved with help exceeds what can be developed alone.

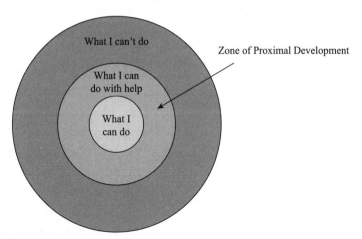

Figure 2.1 Zone of Proximal Development

In a certain writing course, when everybody registers for the course, the instructor becomes a core member and the students as the peripheral members, consequently a ZPD formed. In the process of moving from peripheral members to core members, student writers and the teaching staff worked together within this community of writing practice and interacted with each other through feedback to become more capable of writing in English throughout the whole multi-drafting writing process rather than on a single written product, as is the case in the traditional product-oriented approach to writing. Depending on different task types, different students in the group might serve as the core member of the task. Moreover, the other groups as a whole unit can serve as a core member and other groups of students as peripheral members.

2. Community of Practice

In the late 1980s and early 1990s, cognitive anthropologists Jean Lave and Etienne Wenger developed their theoretical framework of situated learning in which they showed that learning happens in a process of undertaking in a Community of Practice (hereafter as COP). Their fundamental argument is that COPs are everywhere and that everybody is literally involved in several of them—whether for learning, working or leisure. Wenger further developed it at the end of the 1990s.

A COP is a special type of informal network that emerges from a desire to work more effectively or to understand work more deeply among members of a particular specialty or workgroup. Lave and Wenger claimed that a COP constituted three indispensable factors: involvement of all the participants, a joint task and shared activities. A joint task is their common goal to work for, which decides the shared activities, including the process of discussing, negotiating, and listening, and employing tools as well. The members of a COP all engage in some way in the joint task and shared activities. At the simplest level, COPs are small groups of people who have worked together over a period of time and through extensive communication, and have developed a common sense of purpose and a desire to share work-related knowledge and experience. People in COPs grow out of human sociability and efforts to meet job requirements. A COP is typically not an authorized group or a role identified on an organization chart. In fact, they can work at cross-purposes to the intent of the leader of the organization. People in COPs may perform the same job or collaborate on a shared task or work together on a product. They are colleagues, bound together by their common responsibility to get a certain type of "real work" done. There are typically many COPs within a single organization, and most people belong to more than one of them.

The notion of "practice" is critical in COP, pointing out that the group concentrates on learning that emerges only through working, or actually practicing one's craft. COPs supplement the book, and classroom learning of many trade and professional workers to learn how one work in this organization. In this sense, learning is about work, and work is about learning, and both are social.

In a certain writing course, when everybody registers for the course, virtually everyone has signed a contract with the instructor and a COP is organized by the instructor and the students. The instructor has become a master of a group of student apprentices. He or she has to sketch a blueprint of the whole training, including setting the goal of the training, arranging the activating activities, monitoring the whole training possess, providing effective feedback, and solving the problems of the students. Students also resort to different channels to get guidance and feedback from the instructor, their fellow students and other sources. They usually report their progress during peer group discussions and bring problems they come across during these discussions to the instructor to seek additional feedback. Students develop their writing ability and confidence through their interaction with the instructor. It is this type of COP that promotes the instructor's teaching and the students' learning. In this particular social context, students are connected with their instructor by conduits such as classroom lectures, presentations, peer students' pieces, and classroom discussions.

When a learning group in the writing class is formed and a group leader is selected, every member in the group has signed a contract, and subsequently, a sub-community of practice comes into being. The whole class is a big COP consisting of several sub-communities. In the particular social context of each group, students are connected with each other by conduits such as classroom lectures, presentations, peer students' pieces, classroom discussion, and social network tools. Depending on different task types, different students in the group might serve as the core member of each task.

3. Meme Theory

In 1976, the concept of "meme" was proposed by evolutionary biologist Richard Dawkins to try to explain the social psychological phenomenon. Dawkins (1976) coined the term "meme" to refer to any sort of replication that is transmitted from person to person via processes of social learning or imitation. In his book *The Selfish Gene*, Dawkins thinks a meme is any idea, behavior, or skill that can be transferred from one person to another by imitation: stories, fashions, inventions, recipes, songs, and ways of plowing a field, throwing a baseball, or making a sculpture. There are lots of different memes, including words, jokes, melodies, rumors, hairstyles, scientific theories, rituals, religions, and belly-button rings.

Then Susan Blackmore, a psychologist, pushed forward the theory of memetics in her book named *The Meme Machine* in 1999. Blackmore boldly asserts: "Just as the design of our bodies can be understood only in terms of natural selection, so the design of our minds can be understood only in terms of memetic selection." Indeed, *The Meme Machine* shows that once our distant ancestors acquire the crucial ability to imitate, a second kind of natural selection begins: a survival of the fittest among competing ideas and behaviors.

Applying this theory to many aspects of human life, Blackmore brilliantly explains why we live in cities, why we talk so much, why we can't stop thinking, why we behave altruistically, how we choose our mates, and much more. The theory of memetics has provided a sound theoretical foundation for the workings of feedback provision and engagement. Feedback, as one of the main media of communication, a meme, also has a very important and special type of social text, performing multiple functions in the writing learning and developing process. In one class or small groups, when one member has provided a new idea concerning a feedback point or demonstrated a successful behavior in writing, other group members will certainly be influenced often without conscious thought; meanwhile a group can influence the whole class in the same way.

2.3.2 Assessment for Learning

While early formative assessment (also AFL) discourse focused on the role of teachers in gathering information and using it to inform teaching, more recently there has been a reconceptualization. It has been reframed as a social, collaborative activity, aligned more with learning (Black et al., 2006; Gardener, 2006). The emphasis has shifted to the teacher and the students, working in partnership (Hawe et al., 2008) to enhance student learning. Thus, the spirit of it collaborates with the social learning theories discussed in the last section.

AFL is a pedagogical context designed to promote learning. It is designed to provide information about student performance and that can be used to support learning and to modify teaching (Black & William, 1998, 2009; Shepard, 2005; Torrance & Pryor, 1998). Using assessment information in this manner, instructors can improve the quality of teaching and learning outcomes (Black et al., 2003; Black & William, 1998). In essence, teachers need to create learning environments where students and teachers are active assessors during classroom instructional strategies. The latter is in stark contrast to the traditional view where assessments are primarily utilized at the end of an instructional unit or course of study.

Black & William's (1998) seminal work in England entitled *Inside the Black Box* was the first to clearly emphasize the central importance of formative assessment for enhancing student learning. They reviewed over 250 studies carried out since 1988, which focused on real teaching situations. In relation to the cognitive aspect, five elements were summarized by Black & William (1998), which seemed to be essential in the effectiveness of AFL:

- The setting of clear goals;
- The design of appropriate learning and assessment tasks;
- The communication of assessment criteria to teachers and students;
- The provision of high-quality feedback;

- The conscious provision of opportunities for self- and peer-assessment.

1. The concept of Assessment for Learning

The literature is full of definitions of the concept of AFL, among which Black et al. (2004: 2-3) provided a referential definition as follows: "AFL is any assessment for which the first priority in its design and practice is to serve the purpose of promoting pupils' learning. It thus differs from assessment designed primarily to serve the purposes of accountability, or of ranking, or of certifying competence. An assessment activity can help to learn if it provides information to be used as feedback, by teachers and by their pupils in assessing themselves and each other, to modify the teaching and learning activities in which they are engaged. Such assessment becomes 'formative assessment' when the evidence is actually used to adapt the teaching work to meet learning needs."

From the definition above, it is evident that the top priority in AFL lies in using assessment to promote student learning (Black & William, 1998). Furthermore, in putting forward the ten principles of AFL, the Assessment Reform Group (2002) underscores the important role learners play in the assessment process, through which they develop their ability to regulate their own learning. Realizing the benefits of AFL requires that teachers help their students understand what the goals of learning are and provide opportunities for them to have feedback on progress towards such goals.

In this book, a written response is located within the pedagogical context of AFL. These concepts regarding the nature of feedback that have been generated by the literature and theory related to AFL (Ramaprasad, 1983; Sadler, 1989, 1998; William & Thompson, 2007) are utilized to define the characteristics of quality written response in the integrated feedback approach in this book. Before proceeding to the characteristics of the quality written response, it is worthwhile to explore the feedback definition in the framework of AFL.

2. The definition of formative feedback

AFL is used to facilitate learning by helping students to identify areas of strengths and weaknesses to gain directions for improvement (Black &

William, 1998). In AFL, feedback has a crucial role to play. It is viewed as part of pedagogy, in that all good teaching is interactive, dialogic and also part of the assessment. For the purpose of the current discussion, a broad definition of feedback is taken as "all dialogue to support learning in both formal and informal situations" (Askew & Lodege, 2000: 1). On top of that, feedback in the framework of AFL is "information that provides the performer with direct, usable insights into current performance, based on tangible differences between current performance and hoped for performance" (Wiggins, 1993: 182).

For L2 and L2 writing, formative feedback, as Hyland (2003) suggests, is particularly crucial in improving and consolidating learners' writing skills. It is forward-looking, helping students improve their future performance, and hence feedback is also feedforward (Carless et al., 2006). For feedback to be effective, it needs to place less emphasis on summative feedback practices and develop further those in which student self-monitoring capacities become important. The learners' understanding of the quality performance aims for, what success in a task looks like, and what they might do to achieve it is directly related to the instruction and feedback received (Black & William,1998). Effective feedback not only helps learners to evaluate where they are but provides them with an indication of where to proceed next and how best to accomplish this forward movement (Hattie & Timperley, 2007). Students need feedback not only for monitoring their progress and moving forward but also as a means of discovering their readers' needs (Zellermayer, 1989).

In this study, the researcher adopted William's (2001) definitions of formative feedback. Thus, the following are essential: 1) Students are told about their strengths and what needs to be done in their writing, and the assessment is prospective; 2) Information is communicated clearly and made intelligible to students in terms of what they have learned, hence a close link between teaching, learning and assessment; 3) Students act on the teacher feedback and are provided with opportunities to improve their learning based on the teacher feedback; 4) Students play an active role in managing their own learning.

The significance of the definition is that feedback is not a one-way system of information. It, on the other hand, implies and necessitates a partnership and a symbolic relationship which works in a two-way system since it does not count as formative feedback unless the student has understood what the purpose of the assessment is, how it is assessed or judged, and how they can use their mistakes to perform better in the future. This definition emphasizes the centrality of the learner and also his or her responsibility in the feedback process. It is not only interesting on a theoretical level, but also brings substantial implications for learning and teaching. The responsibility of teachers who wish to provide formative feedback does not end when they have given students their knowledge of results or information. However, this is not sufficient. It is not complete until the students have produced an equivalent piece of work where the issues have been addressed and remedied—not until true learning has taken place and has been shown to have taken place (Tara, 2005).

3. Characteristics of good feedback practice in writing assessment

For feedback to contribute to development in writing, it needs to process particular characteristics, which allow students to see the gap between current and desired performance. Nicol & Macfarlane-Dick's (2006) model of good feedback practice in higher education context suggests seven principles for effective feedback practice: it 1) clarifies what good performance is; 2) facilitates the development of self-assessment; 3) delivers high-quality information to students about their learning; 4) encourages teacher and peer dialogue; 5) enhances motivation and self-esteem; 6) provides opportunities to close the gap between current and desired performance; and 7) enables teachers to fine-tune their teaching.

Applying the principles of good feedback practice proposed by Nicol & Macfarlane-Dick (2006) to the writing classroom, Lee (2007) established six characteristics of feedback that are used to promote AFL: 1) The assessment is prospective: students are told about their strengths and what needs to be done in their writing—e.g., areas for improvement in terms of content, organization, language, etc. (also see Jones & Tanner, 2006); 2) Information is communicated clearly and made intelligible to students in terms of what they have learned, clarifying what good performance is and also fostering a close link between teaching, learning and assessment; 3) Students are provided with opportunities to act on teacher feedback and to improve their writing—i.e., to close the gap; 4) Students play an active role in managing their own learning—e.g., in engaging in peer/self-assessment and/or a dialogue with the teacher; 5) Students enhance their motivation and self-esteem in writing as a result; and 6) Feedback is used to improve teaching.

Carless et al. (2010) have argued that "sustainable" feedback practices designed to move students towards the development of self-regulation are needed and that these should be dialogic and multiple sourced and involve more technology-based advancement. They should also involve self-assessment and peer feedback as well as teacher feedback, and should aim to raise students' awareness of standards, and their ability to self-monitor, set goals and plan their learning, and should encourage students to take responsibility for their own learning. They should also facilitate engagement over time rather than being one-shot treatments. Following principles, sustainability lies in the ability of students to improve the quality of their work independently of the instructor. To refer to Riordan & Loacker (2009), the most effective feedback eventually makes the feedback provider unnecessary.

By synthesizing Nicol & Macfarlane-Dick's (2006) model of good feedback practice in higher education context, Lee's (2007) characteristics of good feedback practice to promote AFL and Carless et al.'s (2010) definition of sustainable feedback. The current study proposes a new feedback approach to sharpen students' writing skills to exploit the above mentioned characteristics of good feedback practice in Section 2.3.2.

2.4   The integrated feedback approach: A model in practice

The practical integrated feedback model synthesized two different bodies of literature: AFL theories and social learning theories. Based on the discussion in 2.3.1, the integrated feedback approach presupposes the need to refocus feedback research and practice away from the notion of instructors providing one-way feedback to students in favor of dialogic exchanges in which instructors and students are jointly involved in conversations about learning (Beaumont et al., 2008). Since writing is a dynamic and multi-stage process, effective feedback procedures should be dynamic and multi-stage accordingly to facilitate students' writing development, which means feedback on student writing should be tangible and supplied to students at different stages of their revising and rewriting processes. The integrated feedback approach is formulated in four distinct stages. It is intended to realize what Lee & Coniam (2013: 46) pointed out, "to implement AFL in writing classrooms effectively, two pedagogical practices are conducve to student learning: firstly, helping students understand assessment criteria; and secondly providing feedback and encouraging reflection on it". Therefore, from the outset, the approach is seen as having three main aims:

- To overcome the limitations of a summative one-shot feedback approach;
- To assess students' writing process as well as the product of the learners' writing with a multiple-drafting process-oriented approach to writing and the complexity of the many aspects involved in the dialogic communication between teachers and students;
- To facilitate learners' independence by improving their awareness of criteria of the specific genre and ability of self-evaluation through reflection.

2.4.1　Stage one: The activating lecture

Stage one of the integrated feedback approach is the activating lecture, in which good performance with reference to the assessment criteria is revealed to students. If the task specifications and assessment criteria are not well specified, it is difficult for students to understand their accurate ability level and to expand their ZPD (Vygotsky, 1978).

2.4.2 Stage two: The feedback process

The second stage of the integrated feedback approach is the feedback process after class to help students to identify the gap between the expected performance and their current performance by making revision an organic part of the learning process. Educational research also suggests that feedback is more effective when information is gathered from the subjects themselves as well as others (Brinko, 1993). During this process, feedback is given to students' writings from human sources (peer, teacher, self) with reference to the task-specific assessment criteria related to the goals of the course instruction and task specification, and as well as from computer-generated feedback with criteria embedded into the program. Feedback includes not only corrective feedback addressing spelling, grammar, word choice, and missing words, but also mid-level and macro-level comments that address paper organization, quality of the ideas contained, and other larger levels. Dealing with these larger idea-and-argument-centered comments may encourage students to improve the quality of the larger issues in writing and prevent them from focusing on the smaller technical issues of writing.

2.4.3 Stage three: The feedback workshop

Stage three is to reinforce the assessment criteria to emphasize the strengths and weaknesses of student drafts in class. As an extension of the activating lecture (the first stage) and the feedback process (the second stage), the feedback workshop could help students understand deeper the assessment criteria of the writing tasks after experiencing the integrated feedback procedures, and the strengths and weaknesses of student drafts with instructional supportive strategies related to different feedback activities. Students could get better prepared to narrow down the gap between their current performance and the expected performance by the teacher and fellow students.

2.4.4 Stage four: The self-evaluation through reflection

As the last stage, self-evaluation through reflection is a process of wrapping up the whole learning process for one task. With reference to the assessment criteria, this stage closes all the links of the integrated feedback approach. Students receive AWE feedback with the embedded criteria, peer and teacher feedback with reference to the assessment criteria in order to understand and identify the gap between the expected performance and their current performance as well as produce their own feedback prior to self-evaluation through reflection. They are virtually directed to complete the cycle of "learning" by understanding and engaging with feedback from different sources to inform the self-evaluation of their performance and recognize their strengths and weaknesses that they should guard against for other tasks in the future.

2.5 Summary

In this chapter, we discussed theoretical and empirical studies that have contributed a great deal to feedback research in EFL writing classes. However, some limitations also exist.

First, the majority of the research on feedback practices is done in experimental or quasi-experimental settings; less research is based on a real, ongoing, naturalistic classroom situation. Second, most of the feedback research has focused on teachers' feedback practices rather than students' experiences of using feedback and giving feedback to peers and themselves. Moreover, much of the previous research on feedback has focused on students' revisions without considering what students bring to the feedback situation in terms of their own perceptions and understanding of feedback. Third, although feedback practices are quite context-dependent, they were minimally examined in a longitudinal developmental approach. In addition, previous research has largely neglected the influence of context (Huot, 2002), treating the texts that teacher-responders create as if they stand alone, ignoring the perspective that the meaning of the text will be constructed differently depending on the "discourse" brought to bear on the text by the reader (Murphy, 2000).

So, the previous studies summarized various aspects of feedback, but did not look at teacher, peer, self and computer-generated as multiple feedback sources to the same task subsequently—to account for the interrelationship and interaction between these different feedback processes and to observe the complex processes whereby students learn to negotiate writing tasks and genres using certain strategies. This study will extend previous studies over a semester with a mixed-method approach in a longitudinal manner in an ESL, higher learning context in Mainland China.

In order to deal with the problem presented above, we devised a four-stage integrated feedback approach, which was based on the two different bodies of literature: social learning theories and AFL literature. A key feature of the approach that differentiates it from the everyday understanding of feedback is that students are assumed to occupy a central and active role in all the feedback-related activities. Stage one is the activating lecture, used to clarify in class what good performance is by introducing the task and its assessment criteria to prepare students to write; Stage two, the feedback process, to influence student writing by identifying the gap between expected performance and students' current performance through the use of multiple sourced feedback after class; Stage three, the feedback workshop, to reinforce the assessment criteria, and further emphasize the strengths and weaknesses of student drafts in class; and Stage four, the self-evaluation through reflection, to help students to internalize the assessment criteria for the expected performance with reference to their own writing performance on the basis of all the feedback received.

Chapter 3
The Integrated Feedback Approach in Practice

To explore the impact of the integrated feedback approach on students' learning to write in the tertiary EFL learning context in China, a mixed-method case study research design in a longitudinal manner was employed in the current study. Specifically, it was conducted in a naturalistic classroom setting to examine the impact of the integrated feedback approach on students' perceptions and their writing performance with a triangulation of data collection and analysis. Multiple sources of data included pre- and post-course writing tests, student writing samples, reflective journals, questionnaires, interviews, and classroom observation; multiple data analysis included content analysis, frequency analysis, textual analysis, *t-test* analysis and ANOVA.

3.1 Course introduction

The current research was locally situated in Tsinghua University. Specifically, it was conducted within the context of a selective College English writing course called Happy English Writing[1]. The overall objective of the course was for the students to further develop their writing ability with an emphasis on genre knowledge, and produce clear and effective essays. Feedback is one aspect of the complex interaction among the student, teacher, and contextual factors which describe a

---

1 Since 2007, it is part of a national-level excellent course series, which was certified by the Chinese Ministry of Education for its effective course design and offered financial support each year for further course development.

writing class; thus, it is necessary to introduce the course as the research context in terms of its teaching, learning and feedback provision.

3.1.1 Course syllabus

It is a genre-based writing course, with eight writing task types covered in the syllabus. The one-semester course is 16 weeks long, with 1.5 contact hours each week. Table 3.1 summarizes the schedule and the training foci of the written tasks assigned in the course.

Table 3.1　Written tasks assigned in the course and their training foci

Tasks	Schedule	Training Focus
1	Week 1: Free writing Week 2: Feedback workshop	Focus & potential readers & structural organization
2	Week 3: Application letters Week 4: Feedback workshop	Formatting & relevance
3	Week 5: Argumentative writing Week 6: Feedback workshop	Clear stance & logic
4	Week 7: Writing summaries Week 8: Feedback workshop	Objectivity without subjective Judgments & coverage of major points
5	Week 9: Review writing Week 10: Feedback workshop	Summarizing skills & opinions
6	Week 11: Writing short stories Week 12: Feedback workshop	Who, what, where, when, how, & plot
7	Week 13: Expository writing Week 14: Feedback workshop	Sequence & awareness of reader Responsibility
8	Week 15: Writing abstracts Week 16: Course summary	Academic style

3.1.2 Course facilities

The writing teaching activities in the Happy English Writing course are organized based on the Computer- and Classroom-based College English Writing Teaching Model proposed in the *College English Curriculum Requirements* (2004, 2007). In order to keep the regular classroom teaching environment and a virtual learning environment running as a whole, five kinds of technical support are applied in the course. Specifically, they are Microsoft Word Software, Tsinghua Web School, a web-based AWE program, the Experiential Writing System, and the E-commentator.

1. Microsoft Word Software

Students use Microsoft Word Software to write their articles, which can offer a strong spelling and grammar check function to facilitate students' writing and revising process. And it is also a prerequisite for the rest of the teaching and learning activities in an English writing class based on the Computer- and Classroom-based College English Writing Teaching Model (2004, 2007).

Students' essays were evaluated with the Tripartite Evaluation Model and its three layers to embody not only corrective feedback in form and content feedback from both mid-level and macro-level: Local/Surface Corrections, Inter-text Notes and Post-text Comments & Suggestions. Wang & Yang (2006) describes that the function of this model is to give students all-around, systematic, process-oriented, and guiding evaluation which corresponded to the rationale of the integrated feedback approach. The first level, Local/Surface Corrections, is mainly addressing technical corrections to spelling, grammar, word choice, and missing words. By using the Inter-text Notes as the second level, the evaluator can interact with the writer through negotiating meaning, discussing, and sharing opinions. The last level is Post-text Comments & Suggestions, where comments on the overall quality of a student's writing can be given and suggestions for further improvements can be put forward.

By applying the model, evaluators can rely on the revising and annotating functions of Microsoft Word Software to realize the three levels—Local/Surface Corrections, Inter-text Notes and Post-text Comments & Suggestions. The functions of the Tripartite Evaluation

Model can be realized by applying the editing functions provided by Microsoft Word, such as deleting, inserting, and annotating.

Local/Surface Corrections represented as the ovals indicated in Figure 3.1 are the first level of the Tripartite Evaluation Model, which functions to correct local grammatical mistakes. In Figure 3.1, words that are crossed out mean they should be omitted and the underlined words should be inserted. In the first level, Local Correction, of the evaluation model, corrections are more or less the direct corrective feedback the teacher provides for students to correct form.

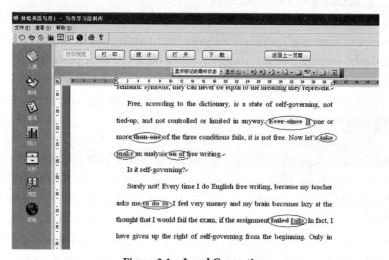

Figure 3.1　Local Correction

Inter-text Notes, as the ovals indicated in Figure 3.2, are the second level of the Tripartite Evaluation Model, which is used to correct, question and affirm for the purpose of communicating with students interactively and actively.

Chapter 3 The Integrated Feedback Approach in Practice   43

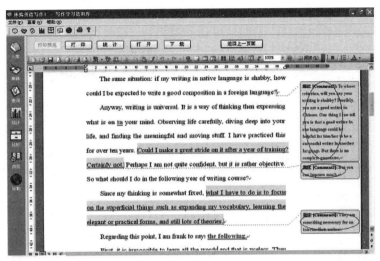

Figure 3.2   Inter-text Notes

In this study, content feedback is realized in the second and third levels of the Tripartite Evaluation Model. In contrast to the form feedback, the content feedback was aimed principally at multiple sentence level issues such as organization, paragraphing, cohesion, and relevance. Of course, there was across-over with form feedback at the clause or sentence-level, but generally, the distinction was maintained throughout.

Post-text Comments & Suggestions, as the ovals indicated in Figure 3.3, are the third level of the Tripartite Evaluation Model that functions as conclusive and individual feedback to help students to improve their writing proficiency from a general perspective. The E-commentator is used to facilitate writing comments in this level, moreover, the recorded oral feedback is attached as an extension.

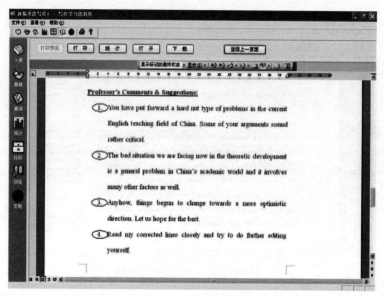

Figure 3.3   Post-text Comments & Suggestions

2. Tsinghua Web School

Tsinghua Web School is the main site of virtual communication for the instructor and students. Students are quite familiar with the format of the website for they also use it for other courses at the university.

In the Happy English Writing course, the instructor can upload course materials and coursewares to the web school. The instructor can give assignments and set deadlines for each of the assignments. The instructor can also conveniently download all the student pieces for one task at the same time with a WinRAR package and upload each student piece with feedback to reach the individual student.

Chapter 3　The Integrated Feedback Approach in Practice　　45

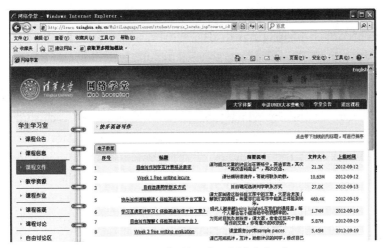

Figure 3.4　The Tsinghua Web School

Before selecting the course, students can go to the web school to read the introduction of the instructor, the syllabus and other course-related materials. While enrolled in the course, students can get course materials from the web school. Between classes, students can submit and retrieve their assignments in the course, and read class notices via the web school.

3. A web-based AWE program—Pigai System

The web-based AWE program applied in Happy English Writing is the Pigai System (Version 2.15), which was originally designed for EFL learners in China. The main purpose of the AWE implementation was to facilitate students' learning autonomy development and to reduce writing instructors' workload.

Figure 3.5　The home page of the Pigai System

The system allows instructors to see learners' writing portfolios, which consist of original drafts, scores, automated feedback and revisions. Instructors also have access to reports including user frequency, which shows times of submission by each student; student history, which presents the performance of each student over a period of time; performance summary, which provides information about each student's overall performance, indicating shared specific domain needs further instruction with the frequency of appearance, and the indication of group or individual weaknesses (Guo, 2012). In addition, the system also provides reports on words counted, times of submission, rankings with the highest and lowest scores obtained of the same prompt indicated, and general comments automatically generated (See in Figure 3.6).

Figure 3.6　The students' writing portfolios in the Pigai System

Students are allowed to revise their essays multiple times based on the analytic assessment results and diagnostic feedback given to each essay draft submitted to the program (See in Figure 3.7). Diagnostic feedback is generated sentence by sentence including writing tips such as easily confused vocabulary, sentence-level errors like capitalization, grammar, spelling mistakes, indication of Chinglish, suggestions for advanced use of words and phrases, and collocation rules. Therefore, the training sets are all produced by Chinese college and graduate students. These essays are then used as a basis for the system to extract the scoring scale and the pooled judgment of the human raters (Guo, 2012).

Figure 3.7　The analytic assessment results of the Pigai System

4. Experiential Writing System

The Experiential Writing System (hereafter referred to as EWS) was developed by the Department of Foreign Languages and Literatures at Tsinghua University and published by the Higher Education Press in 2004 and 2012. It is a multi-functional EFL writing learning and teaching system.

Students can read articles written by former students who were trained in the same manner. The database is a practical writing learning tool for students to refer to articles of the same genres in the database with feedback on them. The database can also score the article based on the results of the comprehensive text analysis. The dimensions by the calculation include token of words used, ratio of token/types, word classification, word mean length, sentence mean length, and the paper length (See in Figure 3.8).

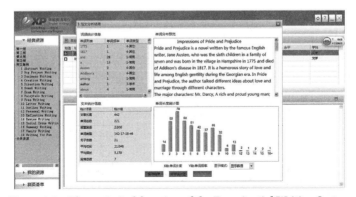

Figure 3.8　The statistical function of the Experiential Writing System

5. E-commentator

The E-commentator was developed by the Department of Foreign Languages and Literatures at Tsinghua University and published by the Higher Education Press in 2010 (See in Figure 3.9). The instructors can upload students' written work to it to be evaluated with the Tripartite Evaluation Model. Teachers can use it as a tool to write comments and suggestions part, for the E-commentator is powerful in generating Post-text Comments & Suggestions automatically.

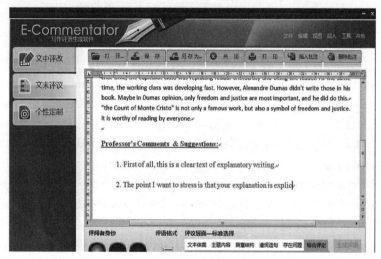

Figure 3.9　The automatic generation function of Post-text Comments & Suggestions

3.1.3　Course management

The Happy English Writing course is applying the di-process-controlled writing training model, which presupposes that writing is first a process of cognitive development. Excellent writing performance evolves from more than just writing (Yang, 2004, 2005). With the identification of connecting cognition enhancement and writing development, the di-process-controlled writing training model interweaves two processes: the process of "learning how to think" and the process of "knowing how to write" (Yang et al., 2002: 4).

Under the direction of the di-process-controlled model, the classroom management is administered as Figure 3.10 indicates. One writing task is conducted over two weeks. The instructional pattern of each task type remains constant from the outset of the course. In the first week, the instructor is trying to activate students how to think about the specific writing task with reference to the task-specific assessment criteria; and in the second week, the instructor is trying to help students to reinforce the assessment criteria, and further emphasize the strengths and weaknesses of student performance for the task.

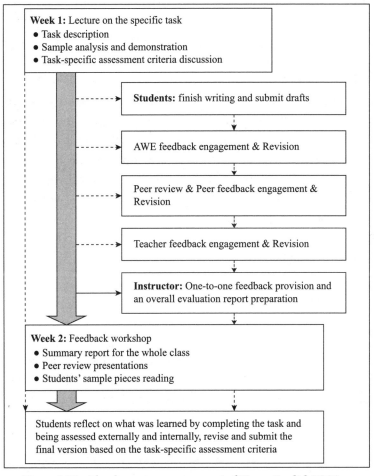

Figure 3.10　The classroom management of Happy English Writing

In the activating lecture, the task description and its assessing criteria of the specific genre were revealed to the students by the instructor. Then classroom discussion was organized for students to gain more information about the writing topic using sample pieces offered by the instructor. Students familiarized themselves with the specific task description and assessment criteria through reading the sample pieces with the instructor in class.

Between the two classes, students could have access to the virtual classroom on Tsinghua Web School for electronic versions of the teaching materials. After reviewing them, they finished their writing independently after class, referring to the lecture on the specific task type and possibility referring to the articles of the same genres in the EWS. Then students would go through all the feedback procedures detailed in Table 3.2.

In the second class of the successive week, the instructor would present the overall summary report on the strengths and weaknesses of the whole class based on the one-to-one teacher feedback. This was followed by one or two peer review presentation sessions to report how their groups had peer-reviewed each other's writing and what kinds of problems or shining points they had identified during the whole process of peer review and presentation preparation. Moreover, sample pieces written by the students in the same class would be singled out to be analyzed and read in class.

3.1.4　Course feedback procedure

In order to match the process-oriented writing model, the integrated feedback procedures were designed with the guidance of the integrated feedback approach proposed in Chapter 3. The objective of the integrated feedback procedure is to utilize the feedback process to achieve an enhancement of the students' learning beyond that achieved through the conventional teacher-led methods. In essence, there were five steps to proceduralize the integrated feedback approach in the Happy English Writing course. The whole process is illustrated in Table 3.2.

Step one: AWE feedback

After completion of their writing, students would first submit their initial draft to the AWE Pigai System for the spontaneous diagnostic feedback based on the pre-set standard in its databases. They worked with the AWE program independently to revise their writing according to the automated feedback they received for each draft. The instructor did not require them to achieve a minimum satisfactory score or to limit thcnumber of submission times before essays were submitted for human feedback.

Step two: Peer feedback

After revision based on AWE feedback, each student would send his or her revised draft to his or her peers for feedback with the guidance of the task-specific peer review form in accordance with the task-specific assessment criteria. Students were then required to incorporate peer feedback into subsequent drafts and a deadline was set for them to submit their essays for teacher feedback.

Step three: Teacher feedback

After revision based on peer feedback, students sent their revised drafts to the instructor, who evaluated it in different modes such as one-to-one written feedback and recorded oral feedback in the Tripartite Evaluation Model. Before students had the second class meeting with the instructor, they were required to have read and listened to teacher feedback in both modes.

Step four: Feedback workshop

In the feedback workshop during the second class meeting, with reference to the assessment criteria of the specific task, students were allowed to have a general picture of the performance of classmates by listening to the instructor's summary report of the writing performance of the whole class, listening to one or two peer review group presentations, and reviewing several sample pieces from fellow students.

Step five: Self-evaluation through reflection

After the second classroom meeting, students were invited to finalize their articles by synthesizing any feedback they received to correct language errors, and improve coherence, cohesion, relevance of ideas, and so on. Once the above-mentioned procedures have been completed, students were required to complete a task-specific reflective journal, according to the course syllabus. Then students submitted the final version and the reflective journal together to Tsinghua Web School.

Table 3.2　The integrated feedback procedures in Happy English Writing

No	Feedback sources			Criteria	Feedback modes	Interaction
1	The AWE			The pre-set standard in the databases	Written	Student-computer
2	Peer feedback + peer presentation			Course criteria & Task-specific criteria	Written	Student-student
3	Teacher feedback	Out of class one-to-one written & recorded oral feedback		Course criteria & Task-specific criteria	Written/ oral recorded	Teacher-student
4	Classroom support (Teacher)	In-class oral feedback to the whole class	Summary report for the whole class	Course criteria & Task-specific criteria	Written/ oral	Teacher-class, Teacher-group, Teacher-student, Student-student,
			Peer review presentation			
			Sample pieces			
5	Self-reflection + self-review + self-revision					Student-self

The central concern in this research is to explore how the integrated feedback approach influences EFL writers' learning how to write. More specifically, it focuses on how the integrated feedback approach influences EFL writers' perceptions and their writing performance.

3.2 Participants

The participating students of this study were selected by using purposive sampling. At the beginning of the fall semester of the academic year 2012–2013, 38 students showed up for the first class (September 12, 2012) of the Happy English Writing course. However, the student number eventually stabilized at 35 after the first online course withdrawal deadline was closed (September 18, 2012). After the second course withdrawal (November 12–14, 2012) mid-term, 31 students remained and completed the training of the course. Three of them were international students, respectively from Italy, Japan and Mongolia, and 28 were from China. In order to reduce variables, data of the three international students were eliminated from the analysis. Furthermore, not having attended both the pre-course and post-course writing tests, three Chinese students were not included as participants because of incomplete data sets. Eventually, 25 students' data were used in the research, of whom 9 were female and 16 male. With an age range from 19 to 22 and an average age of 20.2, the students were from 17 different disciplines whose English proficiency[1] was approximately at the intermediate level as the course requirement stated. The profile of the participating students is summarized in Table 3.3.

---

1 To improve the teaching of English, all the non-English majors are placed in different band groups to study English at Tsinghua University. Generally speaking, there are three band groups: Band 1 represents the lowest English proficiency level and Band 3 the highest level. Upon entering the university and before starting their formal studies at the university, all the freshmen are given an English placement test. The test, consisting of five parts—listening comprehension, reading comprehension, English-Chinese translation, vocabulary and cloze test (speaking is not included maybe due to the complex nature of an oral test), aims to measure students' English proficiency and place them into different band groups. Usually, a large group of the population is placed in the Band 2 group, with a small number in Bands 1 and 3 respectively.

Table 3.3 Profile of participating students

Students	Gender	English proficiency	Major	Year at university
1	F	3	Economics and management	3rd
2	M	2	Civil engineering	2nd
3	M	1	Environment	2nd
4	M	2	Mechanical engineering	2nd
5	M	4	Mechanical engineering	2nd
6	M	2	Mechanical engineering	2nd
7	M	2	Precision instrument and mechanology	2nd
8	M	2	Automotive engineering	2nd
9	F	2	Urban planning	2nd
10	M	2	Electrical engineering	2nd
11	M	2	Electrical engineering	2nd
12	M	2	Electrical engineering	2nd
13	M	2	Aerospace	2nd
14	M	2	Materials science and engineering	2nd
15	M	1	Materials science and engineering	2nd
16	F	3	Mathematics	2nd
17	M	1	Mathematics	2nd
18	M	2	Physics	2nd
19	F	3	Humanity	2nd
20	F	3	Social sciences	2nd
21	F	1	Fine arts	2nd
22	F	3	Medicine	2nd
23	F	1	Medicine	4th
24	F	2	Medicine	4th
25	M	2	Electrical engineering	3rd

3.3　Research questions

The purpose of the study was to investigate the impact of the integrated feedback approach on students' perceptions and their writing performance. Specifically, three research questions were formulated:
1) How and to what extent does the integrated feedback approach have an effect on students' perceptions of writing learning?
2) How and to what extent does the integrated feedback approach have an effect on students' writing performance?
3) What are the factors that may influence or affect the implementation of the integrated feedback approach?

The rationale for deciding on the above research questions came from a general survey of the literature, including findings from the theoretical and empirical studies, which were detailed in Chapter 2. This book took a mixed-method approach to investigate the impact of the integrated feedback approach on students' perceptions and their writing performance. In view of the research issue, the data was collected by way of pre-course and post-course writing tests, students' writing samples, reflective journals, questionnaires, interviews and observations.

3.4　Instruments

3.4.1　Pre-course and post-course writing tests

In order to measure improvement in the students' writing after one semester of intensive training in the integrated feedback approach, two argumentative IELTS writing tasks were administered to the participating students, both in the second week of the course, after all the students decided to take the course, and in the second to the last[1] week of the semester, when virtually every task had been completed. As the original

---

1　The classroom teaching of the course virtually ends then, for the last class was used to organize the "happy ceremony" which is a free forum for students and the instructor to communicate.

IELTS examination required, each of the tasks took students 40 minutes to finish. Students were required to use pen and paper to guard against their using other resources while writing. And later on, every passage was typed into the computer for further textual and statistical analysis.

3.4.2　The writing samples

All in all, there were eight tasks assigned to students over the semester. Among them, six tasks (not including Task six and Task eight) were completely influenced by the integrated feedback approach.

However, because of time and energy constraints, Task one (free writing) and Task six (story writing) were excluded from the textual analysis because they were singled out as course-based writing performance measures. Moreover, Task two (application letter writing) and Task four (summary writing) were eliminated from the textual analysis because their distinct genre characteristics required most students to employ many fixed expressions or sentence structures in their writing. In addition, Task eight (abstract writing) was taken out of the sample pool, because the task design and the data didn't fit the research purpose of this study. Thus, three tasks were left for textual analysis—Task three (argumentative writing), Task five (review writing) and Task seven (expository writing). For the convenience of writing and discussion, the three tasks were renamed Task A for argumentative writing, Task B for review writing, and Task C for expository writing.

3.4.3　Reflective journals

Reflective journals can provide additional personal data on students' opinions on the integrated feedback approach. By allowing students to reflect on the process that is on inside their minds, reflective journals can provide information that are "normally not accessible to researchers, and are thus able to provide an important complement to other research tools" (Halbach, 2000: 85). Therefore, the researcher decided to use it to triangulate with questionnaires and interview data to probe students' perceptions of their learning to write in English. There were two kinds of reflective journals used in this study: one was course-related and the other was task-specific.

Reflective journals related to students' reflection on the course included the Mid-term Reflective Journals (also as MRJ) and the End-of-course Reflective Journals (also as ERJ). In the middle of the term (week eight) after the completion of Task four (summary writing), the participating students were asked to write a piece of reflective writing with reference to the outline as part of the pedagogy and assessment. At the end of the semester (week seventeen) after Task eight (abstract writing), the students were asked to write another piece for their reflective journal with no prompt as part of the pedagogy and assessment.

As for the reflective journals specific to each task, students were required to complete a journal entry every other week to reflect their learning progress and problems influenced by the implementation of the integrated feedback approach. This reflective writing was done after they finished final revisions based on the feedback from machine and human responders in and out of class as part of the learning process motivated by the integrated feedback approach. The detailed information of the word count of the reflective journals TARJ, TBRJ and TCRJ used in the study is in Table 3.4.

Table 3.4 Word count of the 25 students' reflective journals used in the study

Students	TARJ	TBRJ	TCRJ	MRJ	ERJ	Total
1	884	274	457	1,368	485	3,468
2	941	828	696	1,493	1,728	5,686
3	514	648	566	1,097	1,423	4,248
4	283	213	119	914	707	2,236
5	–	–	–	331	946	1,277
6	585	634	505	1,038	1,007	3,769
7	167	594	807	1,527	1,913	5,008
8	484	566	274	1,380	1,409	4,113

(Continued)

Students	TARJ	TBRJ	TCRJ	MRJ	ERJ	Total
9	287	255	353	1,067	1,156	3,118
10	1,212	969	375	2,112	1,982	6,650
11	336	376	–	814	1,278	2,804
12	835	1,093	230	1,101	524	3,783
13	1,196	532	741	2,472	2,193	7,134
14	582	475	387	1,900	1,076	4,420
15	535	–	265	982	828	2,610
16	473	491	343	1,277	216	2,800
17	548	504	320	697	1,182	3,251
18	548	470	558	1,106	940	3,622
19	587	442	156	1,854	795	3,834
20	462	229	842	3,014	1,988	6,535
21	600	507	225	766	783	2,881
22	619	565	754	1,490	985	4,413
23	680	413	145	1,507	1,571	4,316
24	659	659	922	1,223	2,429	5,892
25	407	291	126	1,077	732	2,633
Total	13,876	11,799	10,066	33,607	33,514	102,862

Note: "–" indicates the piece of data was not available.

3.4.4 Questionnaire

The purpose of the self-reported questionnaire survey at the end of the course was to explore the impact of the integrated feedback approach on their perceptions of learning how to write in English. For the above-mentioned purpose, the end-of-the-course questionnaire was designed by the researcher using four question types: closed-items, multiple-choice questions, half-open, and open questions.

The first set contained sixty items that were constructed around a five-point Likert-type scale format, anchored by strongly disagree (1) and strongly agree (5). The items have originally directed the impact of the feedback students received from an AWE device, peer, teacher, and self; the affective factors involved when receiving the feedback. The second set included six multiple-choice questions designed for the purpose of learning about participants' responses and use of the feedback from an AWE device, peer, teacher, and self. The third set was a half-open question part to give the participants more freedom to express their opinions about using multiple-sourced feedback. The last set consisted of two open questions to probe students' satisfaction and dissatisfaction with the implementation of the integrated feedback approach.

To ensure the validity and reliability of the questionnaire, a checkup process was conducted before the actual administration. First, the researcher asked a writing instructor with a PhD degree in writing assessment to cross-check the first draft; she suggested adding more open questions to allow students to reveal more of their opinions on the integrated feedback approach. The second version was sent to the researcher's supervisor to review its format and contents. After a face-to-face discussion on each question posed in the questionnaire, the four sets were framed in the third version. Because of the limited number of participating students in the current study, the third version was sent to the graduate students who had taken the supervisor's Language Testing Course to be tested to see how long it would take to complete and whether the format and the wording of each type of questions were appropriate. As a result of the above-mentioned procedures of checkup, the final version of the questionnaire was developed (see Appendix D).

In order to reduce linguistic ambiguity, the Mandarin Chinese version of the questionnaire was administered to the students by the researcher, during approximately twenty minutes of the second period of the last class.

3.4.5 Interview

Given the exploratory nature of the study, the size of the classroom and the limited class meeting time, the researcher conducted one focus group to further understand students' opinion of the implementation of the integrated feedback approach to triangulate the data of the questionnaires and the reflective journals. A focus group interview is a type of planned, in-depth group discussion that is increasingly popular for investigating attitudes, perceptions, and opinions in program evaluation (Krueger & Casey, 2000). The objective of the interview conducted in this study was to obtain rich individual information. Interviews could provide a deeper and fuller understanding of the participants' feelings and experiences "at a very personal level" (Patton, 1990: 18).

The focus group interview was conducted during the last class of the semester after the administration of the questionnaire during the second period of the last class of the course. The questions were organized around students' opinions of the implementation of the integrated feedback approach and their suggestions for improvement of the feedback procedures. So as to make the participants less inhibited in expressing their feelings, the twenty minutes focus group interview was conducted in Chinese and audio-recorded, then transcribed into English and subjected to content analysis.

3.4.6 Observations

Observations were considered vital to the study. Systematic observations of the classes provided information on the context within which feedback was given and the place of peer feedback, face-to-face oral teacher feedback and the teacher-student relationship. In order to uncover more in-depth information showing what was happening in the Happy English Writing course, classroom observation was needed. In addition to placing herself in the class context, the researcher followed Merriam (1998) in laying out a clear plan specifying what to observe and how.

By observing, the researcher could know how the task description and its assessing criteria of the specific genre of writing were revealed to the students by the instructor in the activating lecture, how the instructor presented the overall summary report on the strengths and weaknesses of the whole class based on the individualized teacher feedback, the peer review presentation sessions and sample pieces reading.

3.5 Procedures

The study was conducted during the fall semester of the 2012–2013 academic year, which lasted from the third week of September 2012 to the fourth week of December 2012. Thus, the data collection process lasted for more than four months over a whole semester. The time frame and events of the data collection procedures are presented in Table 3.5.

Table 3.5   Data collection time frame and events

Time	Events
The 1st week	Pre-test
The 1st week	Training of the Pigai System
The 1st week	Training of peer review
The 2nd week	Mid-term reflective journals
The 15th week	Post-test
The 16th week	Questionnaire survey
The 16th week	Focus group interview
The 16th week	End-of-term reflective journals
Every other week	Writing samples
Every other week	Task-related reflective journals
Throughout the semester	Researcher's observation

The orientation towards the integrated feedback practice emerged as a result of a constellation of factors, including engagement with relevant literature, former students' performance and feedback on the Happy English Writing course through reflective writing, the researcher's early training in learning how to write in English and her 15 years of College English teaching experience, and debates between the researcher and her PhD supervisor who is also the researcher's instructor of the course.

To make this research possible, before the semester started, the researcher and the instructor worked out the assessment rubrics for each task, designed the peer review forms, and discussed how genre knowledge could be used to integrate assessment and instruction to promote learning. During the semester, she assumed responsibility for providing one-to-one feedback for each student writing piece in the word-processing environment with the Tripartite Evaluation Model in both written and oral modes, coordinating all technological aspects of the research, and helping the instructor with classroom management.

At the beginning of the semester, it took two class periods to complete the preparation for the implementation of the integrated feedback approach. In the first class meeting of the semester, the researcher, as the co-teacher of the course, was introduced to the students. Before the first task (free writing) was given to the students, the instructor followed common practice by distributing and describing the syllabus containing task types and course assessment framework. The researcher then introduced the procedures of the integrated feedback approach to the whole class. The first step of the process was familiarizing the students with the process approach to writing as a method that incorporates multiple revisions of the same essay with the help of different feedback processes involved in the integrated feedback approach. The students also received instructions about the usage of the AWE software Pigai System and the Experiential Writing System. Afterwards, one model group was recruited to do peer review and peer presentation under the researcher's tutorial to demonstrate for the whole class how the peer review and presentation were carried out in the second class meeting. In the second class meeting, the instructor first gave the summary report to the whole class, and then the model group did their demonstration of peer review presentation, at last the sample pieces were read to the whole class.

3.6 Data analysis

In analyzing data, mixed methods were applied to address the different research questions: the impact of the integrated feedback approach on students' perceptions and performance. In view of the research questions, multiple data analysis included content analysis, frequency analysis, textual analysis, *t-test* analysis and ANOVA.

3.6.1 Students' perceptions

In analyzing data, mixed methods were applied in relation to the data structure summarized in Table 3.6. In order to explore the impact of the integrated feedback approach on students' perceptions of their learning to writing in English, in addition to use content analysis to analyze students' self-reported data from reflective journals, questionnaires, and interview transcripts. Frequency analysis was employed to analyze closed items in the questionnaire to assess whether the conclusions of the research are accurate reflections of reality.

Table 3.6 Data structure and analysis of students' perceptions

Data sources	Data types	Analysis
Reflective journal	Task-specific journals	Content analysis
	Mid-term journals	Content analysis
	End-of-term journals	Content analysis
Questionnaire	Closed-item questions	Frequency analysis
	Half-open questions	Content analysis
	Open-questions	Content analysis
Interview	Focus group interview script	Content analysis

1. Analytical tools

One statistical analysis tool is used to evaluate students' perceptions reflected in the questionnaire—the Statistical Program for the Social Sciences for Windows (SPSS 17.0 Version).

2. Analysis of students' perceptions

In order to understand the impact of the integrated feedback approach on students' perceptions of learning how to write, the following procedures of data analysis are followed: reflective journals, transcripts of end-of-course focus group interviews, and answers of the open questions in the questionnaires were subjected to content analysis. Then the closed items in the questionnaire were analyzed to extract frequencies and means as a cross-check of the validity of the findings from the reflective journals, interview and the open question in the questionnaires data.

The content analysis with a paradigmatic approach (Goodfellow, 1998) is namely "inductive coding" through which emerged themes relate to students' perceptions about their writing learning after they experienced the integrated feedback approach. The qualitative content analysis allowed a recursive process (Bos & Tarnai, 1999) in which progressively the categories were redefined. Thus, the inductive analysis was performed twice by the researcher to look for intra-rater consistency. A re-analysis was undertaken two months later to check deviations from the first one.

Through open coding, codes were assigned to qualitative data in the first analysis. For instance, this process generated four general dimensions: responses to the integrated feedback approach in general, the componential feedback processes, the feedback workshop, the self-evaluation through reflection, and students' attitudinal changes toward writing. Progressively, the excerpts were recoded into more focused and detailed categories. Then through axial coding to eliminate, combine, and subdivide the codes, themes pertaining to the research question were generated. For example, six higher order themes appeared under the "changes in students' attitudes towards writing" theme: high anxiety, low anxiety, enjoyment, happiness, sense of achievement and willingness. By using quotations from reflective journals, the students' voices were allowed to be heard, which helped provide explanations for and clarifications of both the interview scripts and the questionnaires.

3.6.2 Students' performance

In analyzing data, mixed methods including textual analysis, *t-test* analysis and ANOVA were applied in relation to the data structure summarized in Table 3.7. In order to explore what influence the integrated feedback approach had on learners' writing performance, data collected included textual writing samples, pre-course and post-course writing measurements, scores of human raters and machine measurements of the writing samples, pre-course and post-course writing measurements. In this book, students' performance is defined in two aspects: one is students' revision performance, the other is the improvement of student texts.

Table 3.7 Data structure and analysis of students' performance

Data sources	Data types	Analysis
Student essays	Initial drafts & final versions	Textual analysis
Pre- and post-test	Two IELTS writing tasks	*t-test* analysis
Human raters and machine	Analytic and holistic cores	*t-test* analysis
		ANOVA

1. Analytical tools

Two statistical analysis tools are used to evaluate students' writing performance—SPSS 17.0 and EWS database. SPSS 17.0 is applied to sort out descriptive statistics such as means and inferential statistics like paired simplest-tests and one-way ANOVA. EWS is a new tool for processing textual data which possesses seven functions: collecting, searching, calculating, comparing, browsing, importing and customizing. It can process textual data both into and out of it. Different parameters, such as Word Total (Tokens), Word Types, Ratio of Tokens to Types, Sentence Numbers, Paragraph Numbers, Mean Length of Sentence and Mean Length of Word, can be calculated by the software program in the database. Word Total is divided into four groups according to VocabProfile[1] by Laufer & Nation (1995).

2. The revision performance

Student revision performance, as the first dimension of students' writing performance in this book, was assessed to judge the extent to which the revisions had addressed the feedback received from different feedback sources involved in the integrated feedback approach. Data analysis mainly involved analysis of written feedback from different feedback sources, and coding of revision changes after identifying them by comparing students' initial drafts and final versions.

Every piece of writing in the Happy English Writing course involved three rounds of feedback/revision cycles, i.e., they involved the writing of a draft, followed by feedback from different sources (AWE, peer, teacher, and self), and then a revised version in response to each of the feedback sources. Revisions made in these drafts were hard to identify and categorize during the process of students' engagement with feedback from different sources in different drafts without immediately interviewing the students after they finished each round of revision. So a decision was made by the researcher that only the changes between the initial drafts and final versions were identified with reference to the feedback points given by different feedback providers.

The written feedback was first divided into feedback points. Each written intervention that focused on a different aspect of the text was considered a separate "feedback point" (Hyland, 1998). Therefore, all

---

1 VocabProfile is a computer program that performs lexical text analysis. It takes any text and divides its words into four categories by frequency: 1) the most frequent one thousand words in English; 2) the second most frequent thousand words of English, i.e., 1,001 to 2,000; 3) the academic words of English (the AWL, 550 words that are frequent in academic texts among participating students); and 4) the remainder which is not found on the other lists. In other words, VP measures the proportions of low- and high-frequency vocabulary used by a native speaker or language learner in a written text. A typical NS result is 70-10-10-10, or 70% from the first one thousand, 10% from the second thousand, 10% academic, and 10% less frequent words. This relatively simple tool has been useful in understanding the lexical acquisition and performance of second language learners.

feedback given was considered feedback points. The recorded oral feedback was excluded from the analysis due to its function as the overlapping of Level three of the Tripartite Evaluation Modal.

The first step in the written feedback analysis involved reading through all the student texts to find out the general characteristics of the feedback from each of the integrated feedback sources, which was found to consist mainly of markings on student texts (pertaining to language errors) or in the peer review forms, as well as some written comments. Based on such a preliminary analysis, it was decided that the feedback analysis should cover the following: the overall foci of feedback and functions of the written comments.

The data from the student texts and the feedback points from different feedback sources were compared and cross-referenced to investigate how different feedback sources triggered revisions at what level and for what purpose according to a rubric modified for the needs of this study based on Feigley & Witt's (1981) and Hall's (1990) taxonomies of revision changes in writing. The essay analysis rubric is summarized in Table 3.8.

Table 3.8 The essay analysis rubric for evaluating the revisions

Levels	Function	Feedback sources
Word	Intended meaning clarification	AWE feedback
Phrase	Redundancy deletion	Peer feedback
Clause	New information addition	Teacher feedback
Sentence	Grammatical changes	Self-feedback
Paragraph	Structure adjustments	
Mechanics	Mechanics	

There were two major categories of revision taxonomy, namely the size and function of revision. The *size* of revision refers to the grammatical unit of change including word, phrase, clause, sentence, paragraph and mechanics of a text. The *function* of revision refers to the analysis based on textual clues that the student adopts to make the text clearer and more coherent. It included clarifying Intended Meaning (IM), deleting Meaning Redundancy (MR), adding New Information (NI), Grammatical Changes (GC), Structure Adjustment (SA), and Mechanics Changes (MC).

3. The improvement of student texts

The improvement of student texts, as the second dimension of students' writing performance in this study, was examined in two aspects summarized in Figure 3.9: course-related performance and task-related performance.

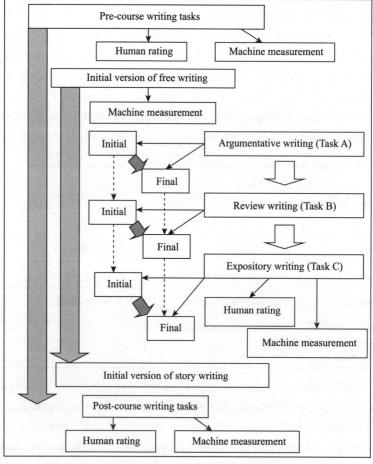

Figure 3.9   A flow chart of course-related and task-specific performance measurement

1) The course-related performance. The course-related performance of the integrated feedback approach was judged by comparing the pre-course and end-of-course IELTS writing tests and the initial drafts of the two tasks of the same nature posed at the beginning of and near to the end of the course. Given the complexity of judging students' writing proficiency improvement in a classroom-based inquiry like this research, Task one (free writing), serving as a gatekeeper and diagnostic task for the instructor to detect the students' writing ability and genre knowledge, was chosen to be used as a complement to the pre-course measure to stratify students' writing levels. Meanwhile, Task six (story writing) designed to give students an opportunity to exhibit their writing ability and creativity was chosen as a measure of their writing ability near the end of the course. Furthermore, the two tasks were chosen as a course effect measurement also because the basic philosophy of the two tasks was the same: each had no prompt, and no limit of time or length requirements were offered to the students.

Specifically, course-related performance was examined from two aspects as indicated in Table 3.9: one was to compare the human raters' holistic scores and analytical scores of the content and the language accuracy, the other was to compare the machine measurements generated by EWS database. With the help of SPSS 17.0, scores of the pre-course and post-course writing tests and the initial drafts of the free writing and the story writing were quantitatively analyzed via paired samples *t-tests* with a view to investigating students' improvement of their writing quality after experiencing the integrated feedback approach over a semester.

Table 3.9 Data structure and analysis for course-related performance

Data sources	Data types	Analysis
Pre-test and post-test	Human content scores	*t-test* analysis
	Human language scores	*t-test* analysis
	Human holistic scores	*t-test* analysis
	Machine holistic scores	*t-test* analysis
	Machine analytical scores	*t-test* analysis
Initial drafts of free writing and story writing	Machine holistic scores	*t-test* analysis
	Machine analytical scores	*t-test* analysis

In order to avoid researcher bias of the students, two external raters were invited to score the pre-course and post-course measures according to the IELTS writing rubrics. Before they scored the papers, they neither knew which one was the pre-course measure, which one was the post-course measure, nor the purpose of the grading. Besides the holistic score, the analytic scores of formal accuracy and content scores were separately given according to the subcategories of the rubrics (inter-rater reliability is 0.963, $p<.05$).

2) The task-specific performance. The task-specific performance of the student essays on the three focused tasks was defined as the task-specific performance of the integrated feedback approach. It was evaluated by two approaches as indicated in Table 3.10: one was to compare the human raters' analytical scores of the content and the language accuracy, the other was to compare the machine measurements generated by EWS database including the holistic scores.

Table 3.10 Data structure and analysis for task-specific performance

Data sources	Data types	Analysis
Initial drafts and final versions of Task A	Human content scores	*t-test* analysis
	Human language scores	*t-test* analysis
	Machine holistic scores	*t-test* analysis
	Machine analyti scores	*t-test* analysis
Initial drafts and final versions of Task B	Human content scores	*t-test* analysis
	Human language scores	*t-test* analysis
	Machine holistic scores	*t-test* analysis
	Machine analytical scores	*t-test* analysis
Initial drafts and final versions of Task C	Human content scores	*t-test* analysis
	Human language scores	*t-test* analysis
	Machine holistic scores	*t-test* analysis
	Machine analyti scores	*t-test* analysis

With the help of SPSS 17.0, the scores of the initial drafts and final versions of the focused three tasks were quantitatively analyzed via paired sample *t-tests* with a view to investigating students' improvement of their writing quality after experiencing the integrated feedback approach.

In order to avoid researcher bias of the students, the students' writing improvement of final products over the initial drafts was measured on the basis of the two external raters' grading. Two experienced English teachers were asked to score the students' writing, using the same scoring guide (see Appendix C), but without being told which were the initial drafts, which were the final versions, and the purpose for grading the work (inter-rater reliability is 0.979, $p<.05$).

The scoring guide was developed on the basis of the TEEP Attribute Writing Scales (Weir, 1990), the Formative Feedback Profile (Hamp-Lyons & Heasley, 1987), the British Council's IELTS framework, and the ESL Composition Profile (Jacobs et al., 1981) to focus scorers' attention on the six criteria: organization, theme, content, grammar, vocabulary and mechanics. These were all aspects of writing that were specifically emphasized in the classroom instruction and in the feedback provision.

3) The cross-task comparison. In order to explore the cross-task performance, the initial drafts and final versions of the three tasks were compared respectively. With the help of SPSS 17.0, the initial drafts and final versions of the focused three tasks were quantitatively analyzed via ANOVA with a view to investigating students' improvement of their writing quality across tasks as indicated in Table 3.11.

Table 3.11　Data structure and analysis for cross-task performance

Data sources	Data types	Analysis
Initial drafts of Tasks A, B, and C	Machine analytical scores	ANOVA
	Machine holistic scores	ANOVA
Final versions of Tasks A, B, and C	Machine analyti scores	ANOVA
	Machine holistic scores	ANOVA

3.7 Summary

This chapter described the research context situated in the Happy English Writing course as well as the research design and methodology guiding the whole research process of exploring the impact of the integrated feedback approach on students' perceptions and writing performance.

Chapter 4
Impact of the Integrated Feedback Approach on Students' Perceptions

This chapter reports the results of the impact of the integrated feedback approach on students' perceptions of learning to write in English.

In order to address the first research question of the study, multiple instruments were applied: mid-term and end-of-term reflective journals, task-specific reflective journals, the focus group interview script and end-of-course questionnaires. In terms of data analysis, reflective journals, the focus group interview transcripts, half-open and open questions in the questionnaires were subjected to content analysis. Meanwhile, the closed items in the questionnaires were analyzed to extract frequencies as a triangulation of the findings from the content analysis. By using quotations from the reflective journals, the students' voices were allowed to be heard, which helps to provide explanations for and clarifications of both the interview scripts and the questionnaires. According to the data analysis of the impact of the integrated feedback approach on students' perceptions of learning to write, this chapter is framed in five general dimensions: the integrated feedback approach in general, the feedback process, the feedback workshop, the self-evaluation through reflection, and students' attitudinal changes toward writing.

4.1 Students' response to the integrated feedback approach

The questionnaire data suggested that students' responses to the integrated feedback approach (Q5) were positive. As is evident in Table 4.1, 88% (n=22) of students felt satisfied with the integrated feedback approach in general, and 44% (n=14) of the students found it greatly satisfactory. More importantly, 88% (n=22) reported that the integrated feedback approach was helpful in improving their writing ability over the semester.

Table 4.1 Overall evaluation of the integrated feedback approach

	SD	D	NS	A	SA
Q5. I feel satisfied with the integrated feedback approach in the course.					
Total (n=25)	0	0	3 (12%)	11 (44%)	11 (44%)
Q7. The integrated feedback approach is helpful to improve my writing ability.					
Total (n=25)	0	0	3 (12%)	8 (32%)	14 (56%)

Note: SD=Strongly Disagree; D=Disagree; NS=Not Sure; A=Agree; SA=Strongly Agree

The reflective journals, focus group interview scripts and open questions in the questionnaire data offered triangulation to show students' positive response to the integrated feedback approach. The following are students' reflections on how they think about the integrated feedback approach.

- Rather than lectures on writing techniques, this course guided us in the process of writing, reviewing and revising. These are practices that cannot be obtained from a textbook. The course is different from those where a student just sits there and listens to the teacher passively. I feel that the students own the class other than the teacher. Overall I benefit a lot under the guidance of the teacher. (S9, female, intermediate, ERJ)
- Only writing the eight assignments of different genres are not that challenging. However, besides receiving feedback, we need, on the one hand, to review our peers' work on a regular basis, and on the other hand, we need to self-evaluate our own performance by reflection regularly, which made me think a lot instead of only writing. (S1, female, advanced, ERJ)

- Though there was only one task every two weeks, I benefited a lot from the discussion and collaboration with my teammates. I felt that my writing ability was enhanced during the process. Every essay was first evaluated by the AWE program, and then our peers, and then reviewed by the teacher, followed by a brief summary by the teacher the next week, which managed to compensate the dead zone of peer review, as we might not have sufficient knowledge about English writing to adequately comment on classmates' writing products. This course guided us in accomplishing a piece of good writing through the exchange of ideas and evaluations. (S10, male, intermediate, ERJ)

The remainder of this section summarizes the themes that emerged from the data from multiple sources, reflecting the students' views of the impact of the integrated feedback approach on their learning how to write in English. Three higher-order themes appeared under the dimension of response to the integrated feedback approach in general: assessment criteria, revising processes, and interaction.

4.1.1 Assessment criteria

The assessment criteria were the cornerstone of the integrated feedback approach, which permits learners to consider the strengths and weaknesses of their writings using task-specific assessment criteria and standards. They could accordingly try to narrow the gap between the expected performance and their current performance with support from the AWE program, fellow students, the instructor, and self-reflection using the assessment criteria. By doing this, students reported that the assessment criteria had the advantage of improving their self-regulation in their learning how to write in English. Against this backdrop, students had multi-faceted views on the task-specific assessment criteria.

- For me it was hard to digest the assessment criteria the instructor emphasized in the lecture while I was writing for the initial draft. However, it was very interesting to find out that my final version met the assessment criteria really well. That is to say, it is very

important to practice what the lecture covered, and then we can internalize the genre features after we revising our article centered around the assessment criteria. (S2, male, intermediate, TCRJ)
- Once I understood the assessment criteria for each task, I had a clearer picture of how to write each task, how to do peer review and how to reflect on my own writing, reviewing and revising process. (S19, female, advanced, TARJ)
- This course does not enhance our writing ability through substantial amount of writing, but through a refined writing process. By this means, we gradually learned the focus and key techniques of a certain genre. The writing techniques covered in the course were not meant to provide a shortcut for our writing, but for us to apply it in the writing of the first draft. And then we tried to learn their applications through constant feedback from different sources and revisions, and came to a final draft that met the standard requirements of the genre. (S2, male, intermediate, ERJ)

To sum up, one of the advantages of formative feedback is that it engages students more actively with the identification of standards and the criteria representing these standards. This, in turn, could help students to develop conceptions of quality approaching that of their instructor and so be in a better position to process peer feedback and self-evaluation through reflection.

4.1.2 Revising process

All the students mentioned that the integrated feedback approach influenced their writing process in their reflective writing journal entries, the focus group interview and the open question section of the questionnaires. Receiving feedback from multiple different sources encouraged students to rethink their papers and revise more. Students stated the situation clearly in their reflective journals, as in the following excerpts:
- Altogether we were assigned eight tasks this semester, and we have done six peer reviews. Although the amount of tasks and

the number of required words for each task might give out a false impression of lack of practice. In fact, every piece of writing was revised for multiple times through several rounds of assessment and feedback, until we were able to submit a satisfactory writing product. (S20, female, advanced, MRJ)
- I think the repetitive practice of the same genre is a good idea. In the first week for each task we can give it a try using the knowledge that has been taught. For the second week, we can revise the writing according to AWE feedback, peer and teacher feedback. (S14, male, intermediate, MRJ)
- Every article I have tried my best by revising many times until I became satisfied with it before submission for the final judgment. (S2, male, intermediate, ERJ)

As the students made recursive revisions, they developed useful revision strategies. This change in their writing behavior implied that most students were willing to revise and rewrite according to each feedback process.
- The weekly assignment has been very helpful in improving my writing, through which I was forced to form a revising habit, which was very hard for me to do before. It is quite often that the revising time is much more than that of the writing process, but after several rounds of revisions, with a strong sense of achievement I found that my article is much better written than the original draft. (S25, male, intermediate, ERJ)
- It hasn't gone too far to say that I have achieved my finest writing product through the review and revision. By "finest" I mean various levels of review and comments—not only from my peer classmates, but also from the teacher and the classroom report. Thus every essay was an overall and time-taking effort. (S19, female, advanced, ERJ)
- I took time in revising my essay. I have learned to adjust the sentence structure to make it more sophisticated. There are various techniques to complicate sentence patterns. For example, switching between the adverbial and clause, the passive voice and active

voice, are among the most useful techniques to polish the writing. (S18, male, intermediate, ERJ)

Due to the integrated feedback approach, feedback was given to the student texts from human sources (peer, teacher, self) with reference to the task-specific assessment criteria related to the goals of the course instruction and specific-task specification, to computer-generated feedback with criteria embedded into it. Between different feedback processes, a revision was built into the integrated feedback approach as a bridge. It appeared that, had the students not experienced the integrated feedback approach, they would not have revised their papers so many times.

4.1.3　Interaction

The integrated feedback approach attempts to take seriously the tension between class, group and individual interaction as it was proposed in Chapter 3. The interaction between the teacher and student, student and student, teacher and text, student and text, self and text, and student and machine occurred multiple times throughout the course while students were learning to write in English under the guidance of the integrated feedback approach. The following are quotations from the students' reflective journals to reflect how they think about interaction invited by the integrated feedback approach.

- This course is quite impressive for its frequent and deep interaction between students and the instructor. The procedures appeared to be complicated at the beginning. Once we got used to it, it was not a big deal to get things done and obtained useful feedback to improve our writing through all kinds of interaction. (S3, male, low-intermediate, MRJ)
- At this course, many interactive opportunities were created through regular peer review, peer review presentations and sample pieces of reading. It is really harder to read others' articles and give effective feedback than writing an article on our own. But if we can make it, our writing ability improves as well. (S20, female, advanced, ERJ)
- The course cultivates a good attitude for English writing through

all kinds of interaction and collaboration, and I am not so afraid of English writing anymore. (S19, male, advanced, MRJ)

To sum up, students enjoyed all types of interaction created in the course because of the integrated feedback approach. Fortunately, they claimed a positive experience of the two-way formative feedback system in their writing progress. Although at the beginning of the course they did not get used to and enjoyed the new way of social learning, they started to benefit from it as the interaction among themselves.

The objective of the integrated feedback approach was to achieve an enhancement of the students' learning to write in English beyond that achieved through the conventional summative feedback approach. It emphasizes the active role the students play in their own learning in the feedback process, and in the writing and rewriting process supported by different feedback providers, effective instructional support, and through self-reflection centered on the assessment criteria. The data in Table 4.1 indicated that the integrated feedback approach is positively functional in changing students' writing and revising processes with more interaction and guidance of the task-specific assessment criteria. As acknowledged in the reflective journals, the focus group interview and questionnaire data, students were satisfied with the integrated feedback approach in general. Qualitative data revealed the reasons why students benefited substantially from the integrated feedback approach in their writing learning.

4.2 Students' response to the feedback process

Since students responded positively to the integrated feedback approach in general, what did they think about the impact of the individual feedback sources on their learning how to write as the pivotal part of the integrated feedback approach? This section investigates students' perceptions of the feedback process (the second stage) of the integrated feedback approach to probe how each feedback process co-functions to affect students' learning to write. For the convenience of discussion, this section is structured according to the order of different feedback sources which was determined by the degree of importance in the students' eyes, rather than the order of feedback procedures students experienced during the course.

4.2.1 Teacher feedback

In this study, the one-to-one teacher feedback was provided to the students in the Tripartite Evaluation Model proposed by Wang & Yang (2006) but further modified by the researcher to a new operational model, which played a substantial role in facilitating students' writing and revising processes in the integrated feedback system. The quotations from the students' reflective journals appeared to offer supportive evidence for its positive impact on students' learning to write in English. While giving feedback to students, besides written corrective feedback in the first level of the Tripartite Evaluation Model, the researcher also provided more positive comments, criticism and suggestions in Inter-text Notes, Post-text Comments & Suggestions, and the recorded oral feedback. This served the function of training students to accept their strengths as well as consider their weaknesses with reference to the task-specific assessment criteria. Students valued positive comments, criticism and suggestions.

- The Tripartite Evaluation Model is an advanced way of providing feedback. The three levels are Local/Surface Corrections, Inter-text Notes, Post-text Comments & Suggestions, which are all effective in improving the quality of my article. Furthermore, it is very reader-friendly and efficient. I personally think it is the best link of the teaching of the course. (S13, male, intermediate, TARJ)
- Regarding the Tripartite Evaluation Model, it is reader-friendly and effective to take into consideration of the micro- and macro-level evaluation. It is very effective for the writer to recognize his or her mistakes and weaknesses both in content and language accuracy. (S2, male, intermediate, TARJ)
- The Tripartite Evaluation Model was based on every individual's writing. It was quite detailed and efficient. It helped us understand the major problems in the writing and how to further revise the

essay. (S7, male, intermediate, MRJ)
- The Tripartite Evaluation Model is very good to point out both strengths and weaknesses of our articles and not hard to accept the suggestions. (S1, female, advanced, TARJ)

As is shown in the questionnaire data in Table 4.2, all the students (100%) thought individualized teacher feedback was the most effective for improving their writing. That echoes the findings from the reflective journals and focus group interviews. Teacher feedback is undoubtedly welcomed by the students regardless of any task.

Table 4.2　Students' response to written and recorded oral teacher feedback

	SD	D	NS	A	SA
Q48. Teacher written feedback is beneficial for improving my writing.					
Total (n=25)	0	0	0	4 (16%)	21 (84%)
Q49. Teacher recorded oral feedback is beneficial for improving my writing.					
Total (n=25)	0	0	0	4 (16%)	21 (84%)

Note: SD=Strongly Disagree; D=Disagree; NS=Not Sure; A=Agree; SA=Strongly Agree

In this study, the researcher developed the Tripartite Evaluation Model by adding the recorded oral feedback in Chinese as the extension of the third level (overall comments and suggestions) of the whole model, which served as a supplement to the electronic written feedback. Students were happy to receive the recorded feedback and felt satisfied with the individualized written feedback supplemented with recorded oral feedback. In their reflective journals, students made favorable comments on the recorded oral feedback.

- The one-to-one teacher feedback included written feedback and recorded oral feedback in the Tripartite Evaluation Model, which made it hard for me to be ignorant of the feedback provided by the teacher. Sometimes I couldn't understand what type of problems I have in my writing by only reading the written feedback, and the recordings clarified it for me. The time of the recordings is limited, but I replayed it over and over again just to have a better understanding of the problems in my writing for the criticisms and suggestions are of great help to me. Moreover, compared to the feedback of my high school English writing class, teacher feedback in this course focused more on the structure and logic of the whole article, and the use of advanced sentence patterns and vocabulary. In the second half of the semester, I used a larger portion of adversative sentence groups and advanced vocabularies, and I have been trying to revise the logic sequence and sentence structure at the same time. (S7, male, intermediate, ERJ)

- I was amazed and happy to get the recorded oral feedback with the written feedback instead of the dead scores we got before. (S17, male, low-intermediate, ERJ)
- It was the first time for me to receive recorded feedback on my English writing, which is so interesting as if we are having a conversation on my writing. (S8, male, intermediate, MRJ)
- I was surprised when I received the electronic written feedback and oral recordings. It was the first time that I have seen such a professional review. The recordings made me feel like I was communicating face to face with the evaluator. From that moment, I decided that I must put my efforts in this course. (S6, male, intermediate, ERJ)
- The evaluation integrated written and recorded comments together. It made the review more intriguing, and helped me understand the problems in my writings. (S6, male, intermediate, MRJ)
- The recorded oral feedback is an extension of the written feedback, which could speak out things that were not covered. (S17, male, intermediate, MRJ)
- Through the Tripartite Evaluation Model, I can clearly identify my weaknesses in writing, with the recorded oral feedback I feel like talking to the evaluator about my weaknesses and strengths (S3, male, low-intermediate, TARJ).
- The combination of the written and oral feedback is quite impressive to me, which is quite effective in warning me not to commit the same mistakes next time. (S2, male, intermediate, TCRJ)

- I have never got recorded oral feedback before, which is effective in motivating me to further improve my writing. (S18, male, intermediate, MRJ)
- I found the combination of the written and recorded feedback is such an effective novelty. (S20, female, advanced, TCRJ)
- I love to listen to the recorded oral feedback attached to each sample piece, because I can understand why the piece of writing was chosen and the gap between my writing and the sample pieces. (S23, female, low-advanced, TBRJ)

In the end-of-course questionnaire, the students' perceptions of the teacher feedback were evaluated using six dimensions, including the organization of paragraphs, content, theme, vocabulary, grammar and mechanics. As indicated in Table 4.3 and Figure 4.1, students' responses to teacher feedback process as part of the integrated feedback approach were positive: 100% (n=25) of the students responded with satisfaction in regard to organization, content, theme, and vocabulary feedback, while 96% (n=24) and 88% (n=22) reported satisfaction in grammar and mechanics.

Table 4.3 Students' response to teacher feedback on six writing features

	SD	D	NS	A	SA
Q42. I feel satisfied with teacher feedback to the content of my essay.					
Total (n=25)	0	0	0	3 (12%)	22 (88%)
Q45. I feel satisfied with teacher feedback to the theme of my essay.					
Total (n=25)	0	0	0	7 (28%)	18 (72%)
Q43. I feel satisfied with teacher feedback to the vocabulary of my essay.					
Total (n=25)	0	0	0	5 (20%)	20 (80%)
Q44. I feel satisfied with teacher feedback to the grammar of my essay.					
Total (n=25)	0	0	1 (4%)	6 (24%)	18 (72%)
Q46. I feel satisfied with teacher feedback to the mechanics of my essay.					
Total (n=25)	0	0	3 (12%)	8 (32%)	14 (56%)

Note: SD=Strongly Disagree; D=Disagree; NS=Not Sure; A=Agree; SA=Strongly Agree

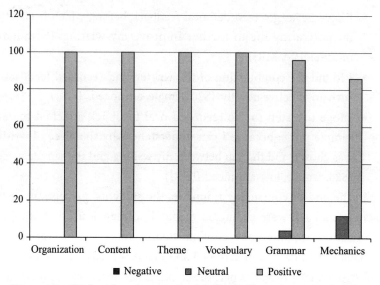

Figure 4.1　Students' response to teacher feedback on six writing features

Teacher feedback, as the pillar of the second stage, was designed to be the most important channel of extending classroom teaching. It aimed to pinpoint students' strengths and weaknesses by referring to the genre features and assessment criteria that had been explicitly taught in the activating lecture of the approach (the first stage) and reinforced in the feedback workshop (the third stage). The students' reflective comments cited here appeared to support the view that this objective was achieved. Regardless of what task was considered, the function of its impact on students' learning to write in English was constantly stronger when compared to other feedback sources, which was clearly reported by the students.

- I personally take individualized teacher feedback as the most important link of the feedback system for it always can point out a new direction for my revisions of the article. (S14, male, intermediate, TCRJ)
- The teacher feedback is quite useful to me, which included grammatical feedback and more importantly structural organization suggestions. Furthermore, the feedback enlightened me to fully understand the content covered in the lectures. (S18,

male, intermediate, ERJ)
- I was happy with teacher feedback, for I always got a few compliments from the teacher before criticisms and suggestions on my writing, which boosted my confidence in English writing right away, although I was aware of the problems I had with my article. Then I would deal with the feedback with confidence and deep gratitude. (S16, female, intermediate, MRJ)

Given the data analysis results, students favored teacher feedback on organization, content, theme and vocabulary. Among the six dimensions, students didn't respond 100% positively to grammar and mechanics. Students may not have had total satisfaction with teacher feedback regarding grammar and mechanics because, as the researcher and the instructor believed that there was no need to correct every written error, the researcher didn't correct all the grammatical mistakes and mechanical errors. Instead, she tried to pinpoint students' strengths and weaknesses by referring to the genre features that had been explicitly taught by the instructor and reinforced by the recursive usage of the task-specific assessment criteria in, between and after the two class meetings for each task.

4.2.2 Peer feedback

Students were assigned to peer response groups which were designed to help students gain support from each other and to avoid students becoming isolated from their peers. It must be remembered that the key objective in undertaking the peer feedback process within the integrated feedback approach was to enhance learning. Of interest to the researcher, however, were the perceived benefits and difficulties of peer feedback from the students' point of view as part of a hybrid feedback system. According to the open question session of the questionnaire, the benefits of reading peers' writing and giving peer feedback was acknowledged by 70% (n=18) of the students as a way to learn from others' strong points to offset their own weaknesses, and communicate with each other to enhance understanding and explore better solutions to their own writing problems in reference to the task-specific assessment criteria. As the students wrote in their reflective journals.

- At the beginning of the semester, I thought it was very tricky to work in a group than individual learning. As time goes on, we gradually got to know each other more; our cooperation also became smoother. Every other week, at the same time we would think of each other, and finished the assignment together as well as improved together. Group work is not only a drive for improvement, it also serves as a monitor to push us forward together. (S3, male, low intermediate, ERJ)
- I would like to give a big plus to the peer-review process. My teammates provided me much more valuable advice than I had expected. And fortunately we could complement each other in different writing styles. (S16, female, intermediate, MRJ)
- Peer review is only a way of doing things, the purpose of which is to learn from each other and provide effective feedback to each other. As individuals, we all have our strong points and weak points. It is of the most importance that we could learn from each other and progress together. (S20, female, advanced, ERJ)

In this study, peer review was required to be carried out after they used AWE feedback individually. Students were provided task-specific assessment criteria in a peer review form to guide their peer review. For the first few tasks, they were not required to evaluate peers' articles in the Tripartite Evaluation Model. Later on, they used it voluntarily because of its practicality. While doing peer review, they formed friendships and supported each other's learning, as they reported in their reflective journals.

- Undoubtedly we not only learned how to evaluate each other's articles, we also gained friendship from each other by co-working. (S6, male, intermediate, MRJ)
- The peer review is really good in boosting communication between us. (S5, male, advanced, ERJ)
- Peer encouragement made me survive the course. (S1, female, advanced, ERJ)
- Feedback from peers was quite valuable to me. And their praises on

my article greatly enhanced my confidence in writing. (S16, female, intermediate, TARJ)

The conceptual rationale for peer feedback is that it enables students to take an active role in the management of their own learning. Students monitor their work by commenting on the work of peers, and develop objectivity in relation to standards which can then be transferred to their own work.

- I adore the peer review a lot and personally think it is the most shining point of the course. And I indeed learned a lot from my teammates. While I was reviewing their articles, I could identify their problems as well as realize my own with reference to the task-specific assessment criteria. (S24, female, intermediate, ERJ)
- While reading peers' articles, I felt like looking into a mirror to reflect on my own problems in writing. And at the same time, I enjoyed the feeling of being a judge of other's writing. (S13, male, intermediate, TARJ)
- As the evaluator to peers' article, I came to know gradually what an evaluator would look for, which was quite beneficial for me to prepare all kinds of writing tests. (S1, female, advanced, TARJ)
- Through reading my peers' article, I could objectively see the repeated mistakes and non-native usages which I should be careful within my own article. Their pieces are like mirrors to me. (S12, male, intermediated, TARJ)

Despite the predominant preference for teacher feedback, students felt that peer feedback had a significant role to play in the integrated feedback system, as they could better internalize the features of good writing by judging and giving comments to their peers with reference to the assessment criteria. Understanding the criteria they are using to review peers' writing is challenging and may require training, but this kind of understanding is fundamental to collaborative forms of feedback.

As is shown in the questionnaire data on students' perceptions on the peer feedback in Table 4.4 and Figure 4.2, 80% (n=20) of the students responded positively to peer feedback comments given concerning the organization of paragraphs (Q33), while 20% (n=5) gave neutral responses. As for peer feedback related to content (Q34), almost 88%

(n=22) of the respondents found it satisfactory, while 12% (n=3) were not sure about it. Regarding students' reactions toward peer feedback related to the theme (Q37), 64% (n=16) found it moderately or highly satisfactory, while 36% (n=9) of them were not sure about it. A relatively high satisfactory rate was found in the responses to peer feedback related to vocabulary (Q35). A high percentage, 96% (n=24), found the feedback to vocabulary satisfactory or highly satisfactory. 4% (n=1) of them responded neutrally. However, the positive responses to peer feedback related to grammar (Q36) are lower compared with vocabulary. In total, 88% (n=22) of students felt satisfied with the grammatical feedback and 12% (n=3) of them found they were not sure about the effectiveness of the feedback to grammar. Moreover, the positive responses to peer feedback related to mechanics (Q38) are 68% (n=17), and 32% (n=8) found they were not sure about the effectiveness of the feedback to mechanics.

Table 4.4　Students' response to peer feedback on six writing features

	SD	D	NS	A	SA
Q33. I feel satisfied with peer feedback to the organization of paragraphs.					
Total (n=25)	0	0	5 (20%)	12 (48%)	8 (32%)
Q34. I feel satisfied with peer feedback to content.					
Total (n=25)	0	0	3 (12%)	12 (48%)	10 (40%)
Q37. I feel satisfied with peer feedback to the theme.					
Total (n=25)	0	0	9 (36%)	7 (28%)	9 (36%)
Q35. I feel satisfied with peer feedback to vocabulary.					
Total (n=25)	0	0	1 (4%)	12 (48%)	12 (48%)
Q36. I feel satisfied with peer feedback to grammar.					
Total (n=25)	0	0	3 (12%)	11 (44%)	11 (44%)
Q38. I feel satisfied with peer feedback to mechanics.					
Total (n=25)	0	0	8 (32%)	9 (36%)	8 (32%)

Note: SD=Strongly Disagree; D=Disagree; NS=Not Sure; A=Agree; SA=Strongly Agree

Chapter 4   Impact of the Integrated Feedback Approach on Students' Perceptions   89

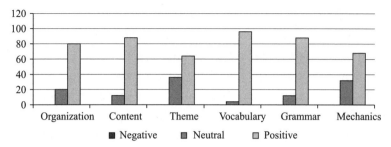

Figure 4.2   Students' response to peer feedback on six writing features

The data showed that peer feedback focused more on formal language accuracy such as vocabulary and grammar, rather than on content, organization, or mechanics, and the least amount of feedback was related to the theme.

Although the overall perceived benefits of peer review by students are satisfactory, they tend to see it as difficult and challenging. This is likely because peer review training in the first class is far from enough. When talking about the difficulties in assessing peers' work and providing effective feedback to peers, the lack of task-specific peer review training sessions was reported by 72% (n=18) of students in questionnaires.

Table 4.5   Students' needs for peer evaluation training

	SD	D	NS	A	SA
Q27. I think peer review needs training					
Total (n=25)	0	2 (8%)	5 (20%)	7 (28%)	11 (44%)

Note: SD=Strongly Disagree; D=Disagree; NS=Not Sure; A=Agree; SA=Strongly Agree

- We had difficulty in evaluating students' articles in the structure and themes, so most of our feedback was on the surface level. (S13, male, intermediate, ERJ)
- The Tripartite Evaluation Model is quite a novelty to me. I really would love to try it. However, I was always concerned about my ability to do it. (S10, male, intermediate, TARJ)
- While I was evaluating my peers' articles, I was ashamed to point out their weaknesses sometimes, so I always gave good comments

on their work. (S15, male, low-intermediate, MRJ)
- As a feedback giver to classmates' articles, I was not confident in my English proficiency though, I still would like to try the Tripartite Evaluation Model. (S12, male, intermediate, TARJ)

Data revealed that group dynamics can strongly influence the implementation of the integrated feedback approach on students' learning to write. There are altogether 10 groups in the class. Considering their group dynamics, there are three kinds of groups in the class: in some groups, all three members of the team are very cooperative with each other; in other groups, only two of the students can work really well with each other; and in others, nobody is cooperative. The uncooperative groups shared common problems in time management. In their reflective journals, students revealed the formula of working well in groups.

- Firstly, it is very important to be punctual. Being punctual is a priority for the smooth work of peer view. If we cannot send our article or review our team member's article on time, the progress of our team member's assignment would be affected. We three all did really well in this aspect. Secondly, communication can guarantee the working pace of our peer review. Although email is convenient but it cannot facilitate complete communication, so we also used short messages. Face-to-face communication is also very important to make our group work dynamic. (S4, male, intermediate, ERJ)
- For peer review, I think communication and collaboration are quite important. We should remind each other of the deadline of the assignment and try to avoid the missing of deadlines. Moreover, communication in class is very important too. (S20, female, intermediate, ERJ)
- To work in a group, we have to adjust each other's working pace. Our group works really well with each other. We keep in contact with each other by short mobile message and email. (S6, male, intermediate, ERJ)

In the focus group interview and students' reflective journals, students also suggested participating in discussions among groups and the whole class in class about their peer review in order to defend their own writing or express appreciation to the evaluators' feedback was necessary.

- I like peer review very much. I suggest it would be even better to allow group members to sit together to discuss over our feedback given to each other in the feedback workshop. (S11, male, intermediate, TARJ)
- Group members are not sitting together when in class, face-to-face communication is seriously lacked. (S13, male, intermediate, TARJ)
- It would be more effective for us to digest each other's feedback if we could exchange ideas in the feedback workshop. (S10, male, intermediate, TARJ)

To sum up, although peer feedback was primarily focused on vocabulary and grammar in this study, Liu (1997) found students were more positive about peer response after a semester's experience of such sessions on a regular basis. Students had reservations about their peers' ability to comment on subject areas they did not specialize in, but they benefited from peer response at the textual, cognitive and communicative levels. The training of peer review techniques and the grouping of students are urgently needed improvement.

4.2.3 AWE feedback

The main purpose of AWE implementation as part of the integrated feedback system was to encourage students' learning autonomy. Moreover, it is also applied to reduce writing teachers' workload by providing feedback to students to improve their essays. Students' overall evaluation of the Pigai program (Q14), according to the data reported in Table 4.6, was mixed: almost half (48%, n=12) of the students felt satisfied with the Pigai program in general, while 44% (n=11) students felt unsure about the program, and 8% (n=2) students felt not satisfied with it at all.

Table 4.6 Overall evaluation of AWE feedback

	SD	D	NS	A	SA
Q14. I feel satisfied with the AWE program in general.					
Total (n=25)	0	2 (8%)	11 (44%)	10 (40%)	2 (8%)

Note: SD=Strongly Disagree; D=Disagree; NS=Not Sure; A=Agree; SA=Strongly Agree

Compared to human feedback, AWE feedback had its own advantages and disadvantages. While applying it to their writing and revising processes, students revealed their thoughts about the AWE program and its feedback in their reflective journals.

- The Pigai system is only a computer program; it never can take the place of human beings. So AWE feedback is quite naturally different from human feedback in many ways. It is very helpful to improve the quality of the article by correcting some frequently used vocabulary and grammatical mistakes. Because much feedback was based on sentence patterns in the published textbooks, I don't think it is very reliable. Some of the phrases are singled out to be wrong because they are not commonly used. (S12, male, intermediate, TARJ)
- Although the system got some disadvantages, it is better than nothing. It is true that the score might go down if we corrected "to do" to "doing" and the Chinglish feedback is quite confusing. However, it is good to provide feedback on grammar, vocabulary and spelling. And some of the examples are really good for us to refer to when we revise to improve our writing. Structurally, I can't trust it, for it cannot cut sentence accurately; it only judges structure in terms of the number of conjunctions and complex sentences. (S7, male, intermediate, ERJ)
- The AWE system is only a technical product. It is normal that it cannot work like a human being, but it can help us correct some mistakes. So while we are using it, we need to use our intelligence to judge which feedback could be incorporated into our writing. (S24, female, intermediate, ERJ)

- The AWE system is strong in identifying commonly used word mistakes. Coming to special terms, it could do nothing. I guess it was because of the limited database. This is a dilemma for us if what we write is about our majors. (S24, female, intermediate, TCRJ)

In order to explore further students' perceptions of AWE feedback as one source of the integrated feedback approach in this study, six multiple dimensions (organization, content, theme, vocabulary, grammar and mechanics) are compared and the results are reported as the following. According to the questionnaire data shown in Table 4.7 and Figure 4.3, more than half of the students (52%, n=13) responded positively to AWE feedback on the organization of paragraphs (Q18) offered by the AWE program, while 20% (n=5) hold negative attitudes and 28% (n=7) gave neutral responses. As for AWE feedback on content (Q19), almost one-third (32%, n=8) of the respondents found it satisfactory, while another one-third (32%, n=8) responded negatively, and the last one-third (36%, n=9) were not sure about it. Regarding students' reactions toward AWE feedback related to the theme (Q23) of the essay generated by the AWE program, 28% (n=7) found it moderately or highly satisfactory, while 24% (n=6) gave negative responses. Almost half (n=12) of the students are not sure about it. A relatively high satisfactory rate was found in the responses to AWE feedback related to vocabulary (Q20) offered by the AWE program. A high percentage, 68% (n=17), found AWE feedback related to vocabulary satisfactory or highly satisfactory. 4% (n=1) of them found it not useful, and 28% (n=7) responded neutrally. However, the positive responses to AWE feedback related to grammar (Q21) are lower when compared to vocabulary. In total, 48% (n=12) of students felt satisfied with the grammatical feedback and 8% (n=2) of them found it not useful and 44% (n=11) were not sure about the effectiveness of the grammatical feedback. Moreover, the positive responses to AWE feedback related to mechanics (Q22) are 60% (n=15) while 4% (n=1) of them found it not useful, and 44% (n=9) found they were not sure about the helpfulness of the mechanical feedback.

Table 4.7 Students' response to AWE feedback on six writing features

	SD	D	NS	A	SA
Q18. I feel satisfied with AWE feedback to organization of paragraphs.					
Total (n=25)	0	5 (20%)	7 (28%)	10 (40%)	3 (12%)
Q19. I feel satisfied with AWE feedback to content.					
Total (n=25)	2 (8%)	6 (24%)	9 (36%)	6 (24%)	2 (8%)
Q23. I feel satisfied with AWE feedback to theme.					
Total (n=25)	0	6 (24%)	12 (48%)	6 (24%)	1 (4%)
Q20. I feel satisfied with AWE feedback to vocabulary.					
Total (n=25)	0	1 (4%)	7 (28%)	12 (48%)	5 (20%)
Q21. I feel satisfied with AWE feedback to grammar.					
Total (n=25)	0	2 (8%)	11 (44%)	9 (36%)	3 (12%)
Q22. I feel satisfied with AWE feedback to mechanics.					
Total (n=25)	0	1 (4%)	9 (36%)	11 (44%)	4 (16%)

Note: SD=Strongly Disagree; D=Disagree; NS=Not Sure; A=Agree; SA=Strongly Agree

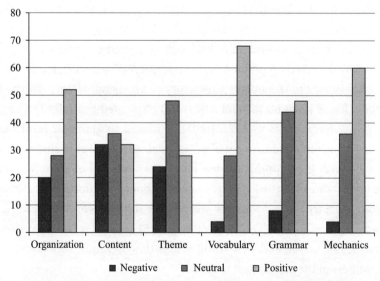

Figure 4.3 Students' response to AWE feedback on six writing features

By comparing the six dimensions of feedback aspects, students appear to view this particular computer-generated feedback software as more useful in providing feedback in formal linguistic accuracy (vocabulary, mechanics and grammar) than in content (organization, content and theme).

Although the instructor did not require her students to achieve a minimum satisfactory score or submitting times before submission for human feedback, students were quite concerned about the summative scores for the first few tasks. For instance, S21 had submitted her draft 40 times to achieve a higher score. But, as time went on, they became more relaxed in using this system as a formative assessment tool.

- In the beginning, I attempted to achieve higher scores several times. Later on, I realized that it is just a program, which can never take the place of the human being. But it is a strong tool in identifying the wrong word usage and grammatical mistakes based on the database supported it. Some not commonly used words or phrases would be labeled wrong because of that. (S4, male, intermediate, TARJ)
- In the beginning, I was quite concerned about the scores, but later on I stopped caring about it. I personally took it as a vocabulary usage and collocation checker. (S13, male, intermediate, TARJ)
- I don't trust the score it provided, but I really agree that it is a helpful tool in correcting grammar. And it is definitely not a good helper in structure. (S21, female, low-intermediate, TBRJ)
- I am just ignorant of the scores, because it cannot distinguish different genres. However, it is useful in correcting vocabulary and grammatical mistakes. (S8, male, intermediate, TARJ)
- Although I revised my article according to the diagnostic feedback, my scores increased a little bit. The AWE software can be taken as a faceless monitor to our learning, I still need teachers' help to explain some of the problems pointed out by it without further briefing. (S2, male, intermediate, TCRJ)

To sum up, although AWE feedback is problematic in many aspects, it is still a good tool for students to use by themselves to improve the accuracy of their drafts before submitting them for human feedback.

Some instructional help from the teacher is needed to explain some of the problems students came across while applying AWE feedback to their writing learning.

In order to probe into students' preferred feedback sources, six multiple dimensions (organization, content, theme, vocabulary, grammar and mechanics) were compared among the three external feedback sources (AWE feedback, peer feedback and teacher feedback). The first dimension is organization. The results of the questionnaires were tabulated separately for teacher feedback, peer feedback and AWE feedback in Table 4.8. Table 4.8 and Figure 4.4 show that all the students (100%, n=25) responded positively to teacher feedback concerning the organization, four-fifths (80%, n=20) of the students responded positively to peer feedback, and slightly more than half (52%, n=13) of the students responded positively to AWE feedback in organization.

Table 4.8 Students' preferred feedback sources on organization

	Teacher feedback		Peer feedback		AWE feedback	
	n	%	n	%	n	%
Negative	0	0	0	0	5	20
Neutral	0	0	5	20	7	28
Positive	25	100	20	80	13	52
Total	25	100	25	100	25	100

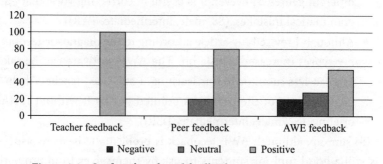

Figure 4.4 Students' preferred feedback sources on organization

Chapter 4 Impact of the Integrated Feedback Approach on Students' Perceptions

The second aspect is content. The results of the questionnaires were tabulated separately for teacher feedback, peer feedback and AWE feedback in Table 4.9. Table 4.9 and Figure 4.5 show that all the students (100%, n=25) responded positively to teacher feedback related to the content, more than four-fifths (88%, n=22) of the students responded positively to peer feedback, and slightly more than one-third (32%, n=8) of the students responded satisfactorily to AWE feedback related to content.

Table 4.9 Students' preferred feedback sources on content

	Teacher feedback		Peer feedback		AWE feedback	
	n	%	n	%	n	%
Negative	0	0	0	0	8	32
Neutral	0	0	3	12	9	36
Positive	25	100	22	88	8	32
Total	25	100	25	100	25	100

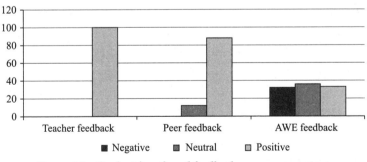

Figure 4.5 Students' preferred feedback sources on content

The third dimension is the theme. The results of the questionnaires were tabulated separately for teacher feedback, peer feedback and AWE feedback in Table 4.10. Table 4.10 and Figure 4.6 show that all the students (100%, n=25) responded positively to teacher feedback related to theme, more than three-fifths (64%, n=16) of the students responded positively to peer feedback, and a little more than one-fourth (28%, n=7) of the students responded positively to AWE feedback related to the theme.

Table 4.10 Students' preferred feedback sources on theme

	Teacher feedback		Peer feedback		AWE feedback	
	n	%	n	%	n	%
Negative	0	0	0	0	6	24
Neutral	0	0	9	36	12	48
Positive	25	100	16	64	7	28
Total	25	100	25	100	25	100

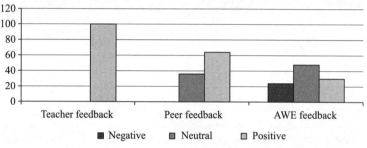

Figure 4.6 Students' preferred feedback sources on theme

The fourth dimension is vocabulary. The results of the questionnaires were tabulated separately for teacher feedback, peer feedback and AWE feedback in Table 4.11. As indicated in Table 4.11 and Figure 4.7, all the students (100%, n=25) responded positively to teacher feedback concerning vocabulary, 96% (n=24) of the students responded positively to peer feedback, and 68% (n=17) of the students responded positively to AWE feedback concerning vocabulary.

Table 4.11 Students' preferred feedback sources on vocabulary

	Teacher feedback		Peer feedback		AWE feedback	
	n	%	n	%	n	%
Negative	0	0	0	0	1	4
Neutral	0	0	1	4	7	28

Chapter 4 Impact of the Integrated Feedback Approach on Students' Perceptions

(Continued)

	Teacher feedback		Peer feedback		AWE feedback	
	n	%	n	%	n	%
Positive	25	100	24	96	17	68
Total	25	100	25	100	25	100

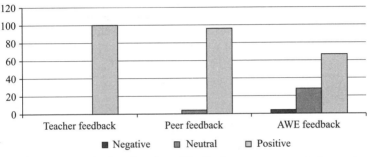

Figure 4.7 Students' preferred feedback sources on vocabulary

The fifth area is grammar. The results of the questionnaires were tabulated separately for teacher feedback, peer feedback and AWE feedback in Table 4.12. Table 4.12 and Figure 4.8 show that 96% (n=24) of the students responded positively to teacher feedback on grammar, 88% (n=21) of the students responded positively to peer feedback, and 48% (n=12) of the students responded positively to AWE feedback on grammar.

Table 4.12 Students' preferred feedback sources on grammar

	Teacher feedback		Peer feedback		AWE feedback	
	n	%	n	%	n	%
Negative	0	0	0	0	2	8
Neutral	1	4	3	12	11	44
Positive	24	96	24	88	12	48
Total	25	100	25	100	25	100

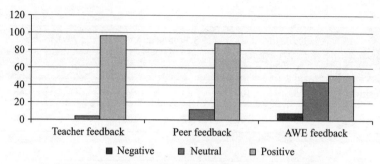

Figure 4.8　Students' preferred feedback sources on grammar

The sixth area is mechanics. The results of the questionnaires were tabulated separately for teacher feedback, peer feedback and AWE feedback in Table 5.13. Table 4.13 and Figure 4.9 show that 86% (n=22) of the students responded satisfactorily to teacher feedback on mechanics, 68% (n=17) of the students responded positively to peer feedback, and 60% (n=15) of the students responded positively to AWE feedback on mechanics.

Table 4.13　Students' preferred feedback sources on mechanics

	Teacher feedback		Peer feedback		AWE feedback	
	n	%	n	%	n	%
Negative	0	0	0	0	1	4
Neutral	3	14	8	32	9	36
Positive	22	86	17	68	15	60
Total	25	100	25	100	25	100

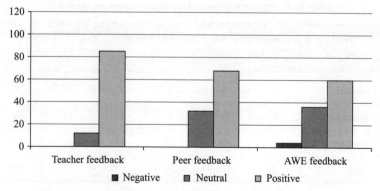

Figure 4.9　Students' preferred feedback sources on mechanics

Except for grammar and mechanics, students are satisfied with teacher feedback on the other four dimensions, while the satisfaction with peer feedback and AWE feedback was expressed by the students at different degrees of reservations. No students responded negatively to peer feedback for the six dimensions but there are students who are not satisfied with AWE feedback for all of the six dimensions. The data suggests that students prefer teacher feedback most, peer feedback second and AWE feedback last. In another word, students prefer human feedback to AWE feedback.

The open questions from the questionnaire survey, which asked students to list the most effective aspects of the integrated feedback approach, revealed that individual feedback both from teacher and peers is preferred by all the students when compared to AWE feedback. As acknowledged in their reflective journals and focus group interview, peer feedback and AWE feedback were "nearly" "partially" or "sometimes" as useful as teacher feedback, and two students would have preferred to receive peer feedback rather than teacher feedback and AWE feedback.

This finding is contrary to Zhang's (1995) claim that ESL students overwhelmingly prefer teacher feedback, but it echoes Tsui and Ng's (2000) result that learners see teacher comments as more authoritative but value peer comments. Tsui & Ng (2000) show, in spite of the cumulative overall results, there are individual variations among students regarding the feedback source they prefer depending on factors such as students' culture or the quality of feedback. This finding is quite interesting when compared to Guo (2012), who found that students preferred the Pigai program as the main feedback channel to human numeric feedback as a supplement. In relation to the integrated feedback approach, students prefer human feedback to AWE feedback, but AWE feedback can be a good supplement to human feedback.

4.3 Students' response to the feedback workshop

This section explores how students perceived the function of the feedback workshop (the third stage) of the integrated feedback approach on their learning to write in English. According to the researcher's observation, there were three main kinds of instructional support initiated by the instructor in the third stage of the integrated feedback approach in the Happy English Writing course: the evaluative summary report of the writing performance for the task, the peer review group presentation, and the sample pieces reading.

4.3.1 The summary report

Based on the individual writing assessment and feedback of each student text, the instructor's evaluative summary report summarizes the writing performance of the whole class for the task, highlighting strong points and pointing out areas that need more attention and further improvement.

The questionnaire data in Table 4.14 also offers triangulation to testify that students responded positively to the classroom instructional support. Almost all the students (92%, n=23) responded satisfactorily to the instructor's classroom evaluation report.

Table 4.14 Students' response to the summary report

	SD	D	NS	A	SA
Q51. Classroom evaluative report is effective for my writing improvement.					
Total (n=25)	0	0	2 (8%)	10 (40%)	13 (52%)

Note: SD=Strongly Disagree; D=Disagree; NS=Not Sure; A=Agree; SA=Strongly Agree

Students' perceptions of the instructor's general feedback report are listed below to reflect its function on students' learning to write in English.

- It is very useful to know the common problems we all have for specific tasks. Although we didn't commit some of the problems for this task, we can guard against them for our writing in the future. (S7, male, intermediate, TARJ)
- This evaluative report to a certain extent can compensate the peer evaluation process and extend the teacher feedback process to motivate

further revisions of our articles. (S2, male, intermediate, ERJ)
- I think it is a generalization of what we have done in our class, on a higher level, I can reflect my own article with reference to other students' performance. (S3, male, low-intermediate, TARJ)
- We can internalize the knowledge of genre features through the general report of the performance of the whole class. (S2, male, intermediate, TARJ)
- It can help me to deeper understand the genre and be clearer of how to further revise my article. (S11, male, intermediate, TARJ)
- The second class meeting is quite inspiring for me to further revise my article especially after we had used feedback from different sources. (S12, male, intermediate, TARJ)

4.3.2 The peer review presentation

The peer presentation was designed to give the student response group a chance to present their process of reviewing each other's writing. It was a chance to co-teach with the instructor. When listening to the presentation, they could learn invaluable information from their peers from a different perspective than the instructor.

The following quotes from students' reflective journal entries show what the presentation meant to the students.
- This is opportunities for us to know each other and each other's work. We can know how other groups evaluated each other's work. We all have different styles, so by doing this, we can share each other's experiences and learn from each other as a group. (S12, male, intermediate, TARJ)
- We not only presented our peer review process to the whole class, but also presented the experience and personality to our classmates. (S25, male, intermediate, TARJ)

The questionnaire data offers triangulation to manifest that 60% (n=15) responded positively to the peer presentation as indicated in Table 4.15. These relatively lower responses might mean that some students do not quite understand its purpose, so training for the presentation is urgently needed.

Table 4.15 Students' response to peer review presentation

	SD	D	NS	A	SA
Q52. Peer review presentation is effective for my writing improvement.					
Total (n=25)	0	0	10 (40%)	8 (32%)	7 (28%)

Note: SD=Strongly Disagree; D=Disagree; NS=Not Sure; A=Agree; SA=Strongly Agree

When preparing for the presentation together in their groups, they experienced a sense of belonging to their group.

- When we prepared the peer review presentation, I sensed the existence of our team. We discussed the steps of our presentation and labor division. Through the only time presentation during the semester, I not only got to know more about my teammates, but also experienced the real teamwork. I think peer review presentations can lead us to know more about each other's personalities and also offer an opportunity for us to present ourselves in English in front of all the classmates. (S6, male, intermediate, ERJ)

- A team can accomplish more than an individual. Through one team presentation, we not only familiarized what we have learned and done, but also practiced how to manage group work in a real sense. (S6, male, intermediate, MRJ)

4.3.3 The sample pieces

Sample pieces were selected to give students' reference for the concreteness of the task-specific assessment criteria and the explicit instruction in the first stage of the integrated feedback approach. Students revealed their thoughts on the use of sample pieces in their reflective journals.

- I like reading the samples pieces after we went through AWE feedback, peer feedback, and teacher feedback. It is a great reference for my final revisions if I come across some good sentence patterns or some ideas that I don't think of while I was writing my own articles. (S20, female, advanced, ERJ)

Chapter 4 Impact of the Integrated Feedback Approach on Students' Perceptions

- Reading classmates' sample pieces, I can realize my weakness easily, which is quite helpful for me to improve my own article. (S12, male, intermediate, TARJ)

In addition to reading sample pieces as a feedback technique, students also take model texts as a motivation or goal to write personally better. The following quotes from students' reflective journal entries reveal how sample piece selection could motivate them to write well.

- In the beginning, I was so confused about the complicated feedback system. I even thought of withdrawing my selection of the course. However, after I got feedback for my article from different sources, and in the second class, my writing was chosen as one of the sample pieces, I immediately changed my mind and became determined to put more efforts in the course. (S6, male, intermediate, ERJ)
- When I was chosen as a sample piece for the first time, I was so happy. I didn't work in vain, and my efforts were recognized by the teacher and fellow students. Later on to be chosen as sample pieces became one small goal for my writing. We need this kind of recognition badly to fight our anxiety about English writing. (S14, male, intermediate, ERJ)
- When my name was put on the screen and the teacher announced my article was chosen as a sample, I suddenly felt a strong sense of achievement. I knew my efforts in the last week were paid off, for students and our teacher would read my article so carefully. (S14, male, intermediate, ERJ)

The questionnaire data also offers triangulation to testify that 88% (n=22) respond that receiving sample pieces is effective for their writing improvement.

Table 4.16 Students' response to sample pieces reading

	SD	D	NS	A	SA
Q53. Reading peers' sample pieces is effective for my writing improvement.					
Total (n=25)	0	0	3 (12%)	11 (44%)	11 (44%)

Note: SD=Strongly Disagree; D=Disagree; NS=Not Sure; A=Agree; SA=Strongly Agree

To sum up, the instructional support is important for students' learning of writing after they used different feedback to revise their writing. The feedback workshop offered a platform for students and the instructor to co-teaching and co-learning.

4.4 Students' response to self-evaluation through reflection

This section examines students' views on self-evaluation through reflection (the fourth stage) of the integrated feedback approach on students' learning to write in English. As the data indicated in Table 4.17, most (77%, n=22) students reported that self-evaluation can help to digest feedback from different feedback sources (Q54). Almost all the students (92%, n=23) confirmed that self-reflection can help to detect strengths and weaknesses in writing (Q55), and 92% (n=23) announced that their self-evaluative ability improved after the course (Q58).

Table 4.17 Students' response to self-evaluation and self-reflection

	SD	D	NS	A	SA
Q54. Self-evaluation can help to digest feedback from different feedback processes					
Total (n=25)	0	1 (4%)	2 (8%)	13 (52%)	9 (25%)
Q55. Self-reflection can help to detect strengths and weaknesses in writing.					
Total (n=25)	0	0	2 (8%)	10 (40%)	13 (52%)
Q58. My self-evaluative ability improved after the course.					
Total (n=25)	0	1 (4%)	1 (4%)	15 (60%)	8 (32%)

Note: SD=Strongly Disagree; D=Disagree; NS=Not Sure; A=Agree; SA=Strongly Agree

Self-reflection was also intended to help develop skills of reflection on work undertaken although some students showed reluctance to engage fully in the self-evaluative activities. The students' reflective comments cited in the next section appear to support the view that this objective was achieved.

- Every time when I compared my initial drafts and the final versions of my articles, I felt a strong sense of achievement. How can I achieve the progress? If I have to put the factors in order, I would like to rank my revision first. While I was evaluating my teammates' articles and revising my own articles, I always required myself to read them several times before working on them. If it is not required by the course, I am not sure that I would do the same for every task. Secondly teacher is the most effective feedback source, for she is more professional and authoritative. Every time, after I read the written feedback and listened to the recorded oral feedback I would be very clear about my problem and how to deal with it. Then the peer review presentations in class, my classmates were so serious about their assignments. I was quite enlightened by their presentations on the task. Based on those inputs, I would work on my final revision with full confidence. (S22, female, advanced, ERJ)

- I gradually realized the importance of communication and exchange of knowledge within the team. My writing wouldn't have been improved without the peer review and reflection report. (S1, female, advanced, ERJ)

Self-evaluation was a good way of reinforcing feedback procedures and patterns of the integrated feedback approach. It also provided an opportunity to renegotiate, in a controlled way, certain aspects of the scoring process. Self-assessment exercises have a cumulative value, and therefore, they should be used regularly and systematically (Boud, 1986) when students are more receptive to change and where they can have a greater cumulative value. Thus, self-reflection was seen as a good investment in the long term.

4.5 Changes in students' attitude towards writing

Qualitative data from the mid-term and end-of-term reflective journals also suggested a dramatic change in students' attitudes towards writing over the semester influenced by the integrated feedback approach. Six high order themes appeared under the affective factor theme: high anxiety, low anxiety, enjoyment, happiness, sense of achievement and willingness. The continuum of each of these themes is indicated in Table 4.18.

Table 4.18 Affective factor—categories continuum

Time	Before the course	Mid-course	End-of-course	After the course
Attitudinal changes	High anxiety	Low anxiety	Enjoyment Happiness Sense of achievement	Willingness

As is shown in the questionnaire data in Table 4.19, at the end of the semester, 88% (n=22) of the participating students claimed they feel less anxious about writing in English, while 8% (n=2) reported they were not sure about it, and 4% (n=1) of them still feel the anxiety when faced with writing in English. Furthermore, every student but one student had a sense of achievement after the course ended. From the above qualitative and quantitative data analysis, it seems that there was an overwhelming change in participant-students' attitudes towards writing.

Table 4.19 Students' attitudinal changes toward writing

	SD	D	NS	A	SA
Q57. I am not anxious about writing anymore after the training in the course.					
Total (n=25)	1 (4%)	0	2 (8%)	18 (72%)	4 (16%)
Q6. I have a sense of achievement after the 16 weeks of training in the course.					
Total (n=25)	1 (4%)	0	0	6 (24%)	18 (72%)

Note: SD=Strongly Disagree; D=Disagree; NS=Not Sure; A=Agree; SA=Strongly Agree

By analyzing their reflective journals and interview scripts, 92% (n=23) students reported that before selecting the course, they had suffered high anxiety with their English writing although they acknowledged the importance of English writing in their future.

- I chose this course because I was not confident with my English writing and I had a difficult time in writing English. (S1, female, advanced, MRJ)

- I was repulsive to English writing before I took the course, because I didn't think I could write well, which resulted in a lack of practice, thus, a vicious circle was formed. I hope I can overcome the fear of writing. (S17, male, inter-mediate, ERJ)

At the mid-point of the course, in their reflective journals, 82% (n=21) reported that their anxiety had decreased in regard to their English writing as it was supported by the integrated feedback approach.

- I always felt terrified and helpless when writing in English. But now I have a better understanding about English writing skills and rules for different genres. I am now able to write with a basic structure and a big picture in my mind, rather than not knowing what to do at the beginning. (S4, male, intermediate, MRJ)
- I feel less repulsive towards English writing. Instead I feel relaxed and no longer regard English writing as a burden. (S8, male, intermediate, MRJ)
- The course and teaching methods have been very helpful for me. I think I won't be troubled by English writing in the future, or by what to write and how to write. (S2, male, intermediate, ERJ)

In the second half of the semester, 80% (n=20) experienced different degrees of enjoyment and happiness while learning how to write in English using the training involved in the integrated feedback approach.

- Writing is a productive activity, and I think no one can completely relax during the process. Even the most productive writer, Shakespeare, could sometimes be stuck with the choice of one word. I believe that when I finish this course, and open my computer and see all those writing folders in it, I would feel tremendous happiness and fulfillment. (S19, female, advanced, MRJ)
- I want to say something about happiness. In the first class, the teacher told us to write happily and freely for this course. And that was when I realized that "happiness" was not just a false illusion in this class. Therefore I write happily, and I write happily for a full semester. (S2, male, intermediate, ERJ)
- I am not sure if I was able to write happily for every task. At least spending half an hour planning the writing is not very happy. But

on the contrary, if I came up with a brilliant writing outline, the feeling is as happy as I see a beautiful snowing day. When I finished my writing and went over it, I felt fulfilled and proud of the efforts I have done in this class. (S8, male, low-intermediate, ERJ)

- I was really happy working with my team, the instructor and other classmates. The teamwork encouraged us to improve together and I can feel my growth during the process. (S2, male, intermediate, ERJ)

At the end of the course, 88% (n=23) students reported that they were surprised to see what they had achieved and were willing to learn and practice more by themselves in the future to improve their English in general and English writing in particular sustainably.

- When I was first listed as the model essay and saw my writing displayed on the screen, the sensation is incredible to me. I even received a prize for my effort. As small as the prize was, I still felt fulfilled and proud of myself. (S14, male, intermediate, ERJ)
- I was really happy in the last class, because I have never expected that I could win a prize as well. I realized that I didn't hate English. I just never took the pain to study it. When I finally understand the essentials of English writing, I find happiness and encouragement at the same time. (S21, female, low-intermediate, ERJ)
- I felt so happy that I have chosen this class. In the beginning, I was so doubtful as to how could an English writing course be happy. Eventually we made it together with the teacher and our classmates through learning. (S12, male, low-intermediate, ERJ)

4.6 Summary

The analysis of students' perceptions of writing learning resulted in four major findings. First, students responded positively (88%) to the approach and, as a result, were willing to revise multiple drafts and form a good revision habit.

Second, all the students preferred human feedback to machine feedback. The majority of students (n=23) favored teacher feedback to peer feedback or AWE feedback, while two students favored peer feedback rather than teacher feedback or AWE feedback. Although the impact of teacher, peer and AWE feedback on students' perceptions of learning how to write is different within the integrated approach. Students valued teacher feedback more highly than peer and AWE feedback, but acknowledge the importance of peer feedback and the convenience of AWE feedback. Peer feedback, though it had less impact than teacher feedback, did lead to indirect improvements and appears to encourage student autonomy, so it could be seen as a useful adjunct to teacher feedback. AWE feedback is more problematic than the other two external feedback sources (or human feedback) and always ranked the lowest compared to the other sources.

Third, most students reported that the feedback workshop (92%, 60%, 88%) and self-feedback through reflection (70%) helped them digest feedback from different sources. Almost all the students (92%, n=23) confirmed that self-reflection helped them detect strengths and weaknesses in their writing, and 92% (n=23) announced that their self-evaluative ability improved after the course. The feedback engagement had been steadily reinforced by the effective instructional supportive strategies employed in the feedback workshop, such as the evaluative summary report, peer preview presentation, and sample pieces sharing. In addition, using self-evaluation through reflection as an important stage of the integrated feedback approach is a necessary process to internalize the feedback from the other three distinct stages of the integrated feedback approach.

Fourth, although the interpersonal interactions between teachers and students or among students did not elicit concrete changes in their subsequent drafts directly, as a result of the multiple interactions, the integrated feedback approach changed learners' attitude tremendously toward English writing, which may help improve their writing learning in the long run.

Generally speaking, students valued the integrated feedback approach, which helped them to improve their writing learning and consequently increased their writing confidence.

Chapter 5
Impact of the Integrated Feedback Approach on Students' Performance

This chapter presents the results of the impact of the integrated feedback approach on students' writing performance. In order to explore what influence the integrated feedback approach had on learners' writing performance, data sources included writing samples and pre-course and post-course writing measurements. In this study, students' writing performance is defined in two dimensions: students' revision performance, and the improvement of student texts. For revision performance, a textual analysis was employed. Meanwhile the improvement of student texts, specifically, was examined from two aspects: one was to compare the human raters' holistic scores and analytical scores of content and language accuracy; the other was to compare the machine measurements generated by EWS database. With the help of SPSS 17.0, scores were quantitatively analyzed via paired samples *t-tests* and ANOVA with the goal of investigating students' improvement of their writing quality.

5.1 Impact on revision performance

This section examines students' revision performance as influenced by the different feedback processes involved in the integrated feedback approach. The revision performance as the first dimension of the writing performance in this study is presented in three aspects: the revision performance in general, textual analysis of revision changes, and grammatical and functional analysis of revision.

5.1.1 The overall revision performance

This section reports the students' overall revision performance influenced by the integrated feedback approach in the Happy English Writing course. Over the semester, the 25 participating students completed 1,026 drafts, 200 of which were initial drafts of the eight writing tasks of different genres and 826 were revisions. A revision could be as tiny as adding or moving a comma or as large as conducting major editing changes to completely rewrite the essay (Tuzi, 2004). Table 5.1 summarizes the number of assigned tasks and drafts that students created over the semester.

Table 5.1　A summary of the students' initial drafts and revisions (n=25)

Task	1	2	3	4	5	6	7	8	Total
Initial drafts	25	25	25	25	25	25	25	25	200
Revisions	204	153	127	69	122	58	93	0	826
Total	229	178	152	94	147	83	118	25	1,026

Among them, six tasks were evaluated through the integrated feedback approach. All in all, students completed 918 drafts for the six tasks, 150 of which were initial drafts of the six writing tasks and 768 were revisions. On average, the students produced about six drafts for each of the tasks. Table 5.2 summarizes the number of assigned tasks and drafts that students created because of the integrated feedback approach.

Table 5.2　A summary of the writing drafts and revisions of the six tasks (n=25)

Task	1	2	3	4	5	7	Total
Initial drafts	25	25	25	25	25	25	150
Revisions	204	153	127	69	122	93	768
Total	229	178	152	94	147	118	918

The data indicated that the students were willing to rewrite and revise in multiple drafts for the task due to the training guided by the integrated feedback approach. They were able to be engaged in writing multiple drafts, and in peer and self-evaluation on a regular basis, which was also confirmed by the analysis of the positive impact of the integrated feedback approach on students' perceptions in Chapter 5.

5.1.2 Textual analysis of revisions

The central focus of this subsection was to investigate the impact of the integrated feedback practice on revisions incorporated in the final version of the student essays, comparing to the initial drafts. The textual analysis of the three focused tasks created by the 25 participating students was conducted to identify the revision changes elicited by different feedback sources. They completed 417 drafts, 75 of which were initial drafts of the three writing tasks and 342 were revisions. Table 5.3 summarizes the number of assigned tasks and drafts that students created because of the integrated feedback approach for textual analysis in this study.

Table 5.3   A summary of the writing drafts and revisions of the three tasks (n=25)

Task	Task A (Argumentative)	Task B (Review)	Task C (Expository)	Total
Initial drafts	25	25	25	75
Revisions	127	122	93	342
Total	152	147	118	417

There were a total of 880 recorded revision changes, and on average each student had 12 revision changes on each writing task. Any revision that was made by the writers themselves—not initiated by AWE feedback, peer feedback, or teacher feedback—was considered to be self-correction initiated by self-feedback. Table 5.4 summarizes the changes elicited by different feedback sources on the three focused tasks.

As depicted in Table 5.4, most changes (35%, n=308) were introduced by AWE feedback. Teacher feedback elicited the second-most changes

(30%, n=262), self-correction (21%, n=191) the third, and peer feedback (14%, n=119) the least.

Table 5.4 Revisions elicited by feedback sources (n=25)

	Feedback sources				
	Teacher	Student			Total
		Peer	Self		
	Teacher feedback	Peer feedback	Self-feedback	AWE feedback	
Revisions	262	119	191	308	880
Change portion (%)	30	14	21	35	100

Collectively, 56% (n=499) of the changes, 35% based on AWE feedback plus 21% based on self-correction, resulted from the students' own decisions. Meanwhile, 70% (n=618) of the changes, 14% on peer feedback plus 35% on AWE feedback and 21% for self-correction, resulted from the help of their fellow students and the AWE software. Teacher feedback made up the remaining 30% (n=262) of changes. The integrated feedback approach succeeded in creating a feedback-rich environment for individualized learning, with students solving their own difficulties in revision and instructors having fostered students' autonomy without total dependence on teachers.

5.1.3 The grammatical and functional analysis of revisions

In order to shed light on students' revision behaviors, two major revision operations on 25 participating students' texts (e.g., size and function of revision) were analyzed. According to the rubric detailed in Figure 5.3, the initial drafts and final versions of the three tasks were compared to identify the changes with reference to the feedback from different sources for the specific task.

1. The size of revision

The first cross-element analysis was a comparison of the different feedback processes in reference to the different sizes of revisions, which refer to the grammatical unit of changes including word, phrase, clause, sentence, paragraph and mechanics of a text.

After comparing the initial drafts with the final versions, the revisions made by the students that eventually remained in their final versions according to different feedback sources were coded. For the convenience of discussion, the three levels of phrase, clause and sentence are combined as syntactic levels when reporting the results. The purpose of this analysis was to illuminate the different feedback sources with reference to the grammatical levels of the changes made. Table 5.5 summarizes the data from this comparison. As indicated in Table 5.5, among all the changes, the most changes (46%, n=402) happened at the word level. Then, changes at the syntactic level (40%, n=349) ranked second, mechanic level changes (8%, n=71) third, and the paragraph level (6%, n=58) last.

Table 5.5 Each level of revision elicited by feedback sources (n=25)

Size	Word	Syntax	Paragraph	Mechanics	Total
Revisions	402	349	58	71	880
Change portion (%)	46	40	6	8	100

As is shown in Table 5.6, at the word level, AWE feedback introduced more changes (50%, n=200) than other feedback sources. Teacher feedback elicited 26.5% (n=103) of the changes and ranked second. Then, peer feedback was the third, which stimulated 20% (n=82) of the word level changes. Self-feedback (3.5%, n=17) ranked last at the word level.

At the syntactic level, self-correction (41%, n=146) ranked first. Teacher feedback closely followed as the second (34%, n=117). AWE feedback (19%, n=65) came in third. Peer feedback (6%, n=21) resulted in the fewest revisions at the syntactic level. At the paragraph level, teacher feedback and self-feedback ranked neck in neck (45%, n=26). AWE feedback (7%, n=4) came in third, and peer feedback (3%, n=2) fourth. At the mechanics level, AWE feedback (55%, n=33) came in first. Teacher feedback (22%, n=16) and peer feedback (20%, n=14) elicited nearly the same amount of changes in mechanics. Self-feedback (3%, n=2) happened least often at this level.

Table 5.6 Each level of revision elicited by feedback sources and percentage (n=25)

Size	Word		Syntactic		Paragraph		Mechanics	
	n	%	n	%	n	%	n	%
AWE feedback	200	50	65	19	4	7	39	55
Peer feedback	82	20	21	6	2	3	14	20
Teacher feedback	103	26.5	117	34	26	45	16	22
Self-feedback	17	3.5	146	41	26	45	2	3
Total	402	100	349	100	58	100	71	100

This suggests that individual writers activated revision at larger writing-level units after receiving feedback from different feedback sources. Teacher feedback, as the second, has more effect at the paragraph level, but it also has a strong effect on revisions made at the word level, syntactic and mechanical levels. The AWE program is stronger in giving feedback at the word and mechanics levels and weaker at the syntactic and paragraph levels. Compared with other feedback sources, changes introduced by peer feedback happened least at all levels. Besides the word level, peer feedback resulted in the fewest revisions at other levels.

2. The function of revision

The second cross-analysis was a comparison of the different feedback sources in reference to the different functions of revisions. In other words, this comparison identifies the relationship between the feedback sources and the purpose for the revisions made. It included Meaning Clarification (MC), Redundancy Deletion (RD), Information Addition (IA), Grammatical Changes (GC), Structure Adjustment (SA), and Mechanics Exchange (ME).

After comparing the initial drafts with the final versions, the revisions made by the students that eventually remained in their final versions according to different feedback sources were coded using Faigley & Witte's (1981) taxonomy, which categorizes revisions as either surface changes (local changes altering the surface structure but not adding new or deleting old information) or meaning changes (global changes affecting the information presented in the text by either adding, deleting, or rearranging the ideas). Table 5.7 summarizes the data from this comparison.

Table 5.7 Each type of revision elicited by feedback sources (n=25)

Function	Meaning changes	Surface changes	Total
Revisions	425	455	880
Change portion (%)	48	52	100

Altogether, the surface changes (52%, n=455) were slightly more than the meaning changes (48%, n=425) by 4%. That suggests that the integrated feedback approach could launch revisions on students' writing both in language accuracy and content. Specifically, as indicated in Table 5.8, AWE feedback (44%, n=198) ranked first and teacher feedback (27%, n=127) ranked second in providing stimulus for surface changes, while self-feedback (36%, n=151) ranked first and teacher feedback (32%, n=135) ranked second in providing stimulus for meaning changes. Peer feedback was still the weakest in providing meaning changes (7%, n=29), and ranked second-to-last (20%, n=90) in providing surface changes.

Table 5.8 Each type of revision elicited by feedback sources (n=25)

Function	Meaning changes		Surface changes	
	n	%	n	%
AWE feedback	110	25	198	44
Peer feedback	29	7	90	20
Teacher feedback	135	32	127	27
Self-feedback	151	36	40	9
Total	425	100	455	100

The data indicated that self-feedback was the strongest in meaning changes, teacher feedback was balanced in eliciting both meaning and surface changes, AWE feedback was the strongest in leading surface changes, and peer feedback was weakest in both kinds of changes.

As depicted in Table 5.9, at the meaning change level, self-correction is strongest in adding new information (69%, n=99); teacher feedback was still balanced in intended meaning clarification (30%, n=56), redundant meaning deletion (56%, n=54), and new information addition (17%, n=25); peer feedback ranked second in deleting meaning redundancy in meaning (19%, n=18); AWE feedback was the strongest in intended meaning clarification (41%, n=76). At the surface change level, teacher feedback (59%, n=47) stimulated the most changes in structure; self-correction at 28% (n=22) in structure; AWE feedback (50%, n=152) was strongest in grammatical changes, and peer feedback (24%, n=72) was second in grammatical changes.

Table 5.9 Each type of revision elicited by feedback sources (n=25)

Function	Meaning changes						Surface changes					
	MC		RD		IA		GC		SA		ME	
	n	%	n	%	n	%	n	%	n	%	n	%
AWE feedback	76	41	16	17	18	13	152	50	7	9	39	55
Peer feedback	9	5	18	19	2	1	72	24	4	5	14	20
Teacher feedback	56	30	54	56	25	17	64	21	47	58	16	22
Self-feedback	44	24	8	8	99	69	16	5	22	28	2	3
Total	185	100	96	100	144	100	304	100	80	100	71	100

Note: MC=Meaning Clarification; RD=Redundancy Deletion; IA=Information Addition; GC=Grammatical Changes; SA= Structural Adjustment; ME=Mechanics Exchange.

This suggests that students themselves activated more revisions in new information added at the meaning change level after receiving multi-sourced feedback. Teacher feedback is much functional in deleting redundancy and structure adjustment at the surface change level. AWE feedback is stronger in giving feedback on meaning clarification at the meaning changes level and grammatical changes at the surface change level. Changes introduced by peer feedback were weaker at all levels.

5.2 Impact on writing improvement

After acknowledging how the students made use of feedback from different feedback sources in their revisions, the quality of their texts needed to be examined to testify to students' writing performance improvement. As the second dimension of students' writing performance in this study, writing improvement was examined in two aspects: course-related performance and task-related performance.

5.2.1 The course-related performance

In order to verify whether or not students' writing quality improved after they experienced the integrated feedback approach over the semester, students' course-related performance was examined from two aspects: one was to compare the writing quality of two pre-course and post-course IELTS writing tasks, and the other was to compare writing quality of the first task (free writing) and the sixth task (story writing) within the course.

1. The pre-course and post-course IELTS writing tasks

The writing quality of the pre-course and post-course IELTS writing tasks was specifically examined from two approaches via paired samples *t-tests* with a view to investigating students' improvement in their writing quality after experiencing the integrated feedback approach over a semester: one was to compare the human raters' holistic scores and analytical scores of content and language accuracy; the other was to compare the machine measurements generated by ESW database.

1) The human raters' measurement. Table 5.10 and Figure 5.1 present that the results of the paired samples *t-tests* are significant. As is shown

in Table 5.10 and Figure 5.1, the participants significantly improved their performance in both content, with an average of 6.3 (SD=1.09) in the post-test and 5.86 in the pre-test (SD=0.96), t (24)=−2.431, p=0.023 (two-tailed), and linguistic accuracy, with an average of 6.18 (SD=0.86) in the post-test and 5.86 (SD=0.85) in the pre-test, t (24)=−2.975, p=0.007 (two-tailed). Furthermore, the scores given holistically also increased significantly from a mean of 5.74 (SD=0.94) in the pre-test to 6.10 (SD=0.80), t (24)=−2.221, p=0.036 (two-tailed) in the post-test.

Table 5.10　The *t-tests* results of scores (pre-test vs. post-test)

Category	Mean of pre-test	Mean of post-test	t-value	Significance
Content	5.86±0.19 (0.96)	6.3±0.22 (1.09)	−2.431	0.023*
Language	5.86±0.17 (0.85)	6.18±0.17 (0.86)	−2.975	0.007*
Total	5.74±0.19 (0.94)	6.10±0.16 (0.80)	−2.221	0.036*

Note: The table shows the results of mean (±SE). The numbers in the parentheses are the standard deviation of each item. * represents significance and the significant effects (p<0.05).

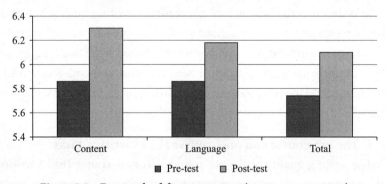

Figure 5.1　Bar graph of the mean scores (pre-test vs. post-test)

2) The machine measurement. To check the detailed changes from the pre-test to the post-test, we also ran a paired samples *t-tests* of each item of writing assessed by EWS database. As Table 5.11 and Figure 5.2 show, the participants write longer in the post-test (M=270.56, SD=56.25) than in the pre-test (M=238.12, SD=63.54), t (24)=−2.957, p=0.007 (two-tailed). And the number of total words

was 12.32 more on average in the post-test (M=139.72, SD=22.40) than in the pre-test (M=127.40, SD=25.77), t (24)=–2.754, p=0.011 (two-tailed). However, the sentence length [t (24)=–1.432, *ns*] did not significantly differ between the two tests. The secondary most frequent thousand words of English significantly increased, with an average of 13.00 (SD=3.66) in the post-test and 10.68 (SD=4.70) in the pre-test, t (24)=–2.781, p=0.010 (two-tailed). The remainder which was not found on the other list was almost two times more in the post-test (M=13.16, SD=5.13) than in the pre-test (M=7.72, SD=3.75), t (24)=–5.476, p=0.000 (two-tailed). In addition, the participants used longer words in the post-test (M=4.69, SD=0.23) than in the pre-test (M=4.56, SD=4.56), t (24)=–3. 079, p=0.005 (two-tailed). However, other vocabulary use such as the most frequent thousand words [t (24)=–0.975, *ns*], the academic words of English [t (24)=–1.581, *ns*] and repetition ratio [t (24)=–2.035, *ns*] showed no significant change between the two tests.

Table 5.11 The *t-test* results of EWS measurements (pre-test vs. post-test)

Category	Mean of pre-test	Mean of post-test	t-value	Significance
Paper length	238.12±12.71 (63.54)	270.56±11.25 (56.25)	–2.957	0.007*
Sentence length	16.99±0.58 (2.89)	17.45±0.44 (3.29)	–1.432	0.165
Total word	127.40±5.15 (25.77)	139.72±4.48 (22.40)	–2.754	0.011*
MF 1,000	101.20±3.94 (19.68)	104.76±3.42 (17.11)	–0.975	0.339
SMF	10.68±0.94 (4.70)	13.00±0.73 (3.66)	–2.781	0.010*
AWL	7.80±0.72 (3.59)	8.80±0.75 (3.74)	–1.581	0.127
Remainder	7.72±0.75 (3.75)	13.16±1.03 (5.13)	–5.476	0.000*
Repetition ratio	1.85±0.04 (0.22)	1.93±0.05 (0.23)	–2.035	0.053
Word length	4.56±0.05 (0.26)	4.69±0.05 (0.23)	–3.079	0.005*

Note: The table shows the results of mean (±SE). The numbers in the parentheses are the standard deviation of each item. * represents significance and the significant effects (p<0.05).

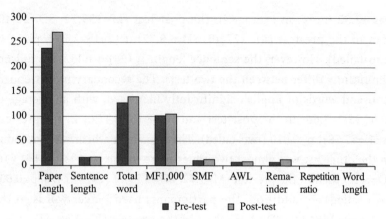

Figure 5.2 EWS measurements means (pre-test vs. post-test)

2. Task one and Task six

Given the complexity of judging student writing in a classroom-based inquiry like this research, two tasks within the course were chosen as course-related writing performance measures to complement the pre-course and post-course writing measures. One was Task one (free writing), which served as a gatekeeper and diagnostic task for the instructor to detect the students' writing ability and genre knowledge. The other one was Task six (story writing), which was designed to give students an opportunity to exhibit their writing ability. They were chosen because the basic philosophy of the two tasks was the same, with no limit of time, length requirement or specific prompts offered to the students. To serve the research purpose, we only need to measure the initial drafts of the two tasks by comparing the results generated by the ESW database via paired samples *t-tests*.

As Table 5.12 and Figure 5.3 show, the participants write three times longer papers in story writing (M=612.64, SD=210.57) than in free writing (M=296, SD=105.22), t (24)=-7.781, p=0.000 (two-tailed). However, sentence length significantly decreased, with an average of 16.75 (SD=3.40) in free writing and 12.41 (SD=2.46) in story writing, t (24) =5.766, p=0.000 (two-tailed).

It is apparent that the integrated feedback approach had a significant effect on the participants' vocabulary choice. The number of total words increased by more than 100 in story writing (M=274.08, SD=83) than in free writing (M=159.88, SD=46.18), t (24)=–7.651, p=0.000 (two-tailed). The use of the most frequent thousand words of English also increased substantially from free writing (M=121.44, SD=35.99) to story writing (M=201.44, SD=53.80), t (24)=–7.514, p=0.000 (two-tailed). The second most frequent thousand words of English was more than two times more in story writing (M=32.92, SD=16.48) than those in free writing (M=13.28, SD=5.27), t (24)=–7.439, p=0.000 (two-tailed). The remainder which is not found on the other lists also increases significantly, with an average of 17.68 (SD=9.72) in free writing and 32.04 (SD=17.34) in story writing, t (24)=–4.951, p=0.000 (two-tailed). The repetition ratio of vocabulary use also significantly increased, with an average of 1.83 (SD=1.83) in free writing and 2.22 (SD=0.25) in story writing, t (24)= –5.963, p=0.000 (two-tailed). Meanwhile, the number of academic words of English also increased, but the difference was not statistically significant [t (24) =–0.142, *ns*]. However, the word length decreased a little, with an average of 4.5 (SD=0.21) in free writing and 4.13 (SD=0.20) in story writing, t (24)=4.874, p=0.000.

Table 5.12 The *t-test* results of EWS measurements (free writing vs. story writing)

Category	Mean of free writing	Mean of story writing	t-value	Significance
Paper length	296±21.04 (105.22)	612.64±42.11 (210.57)	–7.718	0.000*
Sentence length	16.75±0.68 (3.40)	12.41±0.49 (2.46)	5.766	0.000*
Total word	159.88±9.24 (46.18)	274.08±16.60 (83)	–7.651	0.000*
MF 1,000	121.44±7.20 (35.99)	201.44±10.76 (53.80)	–7.514	0.000*
SMF	13.28±1.05 (5.27)	32.92±3.30 (16.48)	–7.439	0.000*
AWL	7.48±1.07 (5.37)	7.68±0.96 (4.78)	–0.142	0.888
Remainder	17.68±1.94 (9.72)	32.04±3.47 (17.34)	–4.951	0.000*
Repetition ratio	1.83±0.04 (0.21)	2.22±0.05 (0.25)	–5.963	0.000*
Word length	4.50±0.06 (0.32)	4.13±0.04 (0.20)	4.874	0.000*

Notes: The table shows the results of mean (±SE). The numbers in the parentheses are the standard deviation of each item. * represents significance and the significant effects (p<0.05).

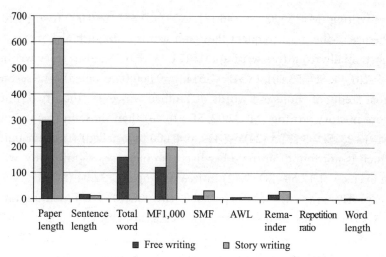

Figure 5.3　EWS measurements (free writing vs. story writing)

To sum up, there is a significant improvement in content, language and total scores from pre-test to post-test; and there is a significant improvement in EWS measurements from the initial drafts of free writing (Task one) to those of story writing (Task six). Thus, the integrated feedback approach has a positive effect on students' course-related performance.

5.2.2　The task-related performance

In order to explore the impact of the integrated feedback approach on students' task-related performance, comparative measurements were employed in two ways: one was within task comparison, in which the quality of the initial drafts and the final versions of each selected task were compared via paired samples *t-tests*; the other was across task comparison via one-way ANOVA.

1. Task A

Table 5.13 and Figure 5.4 show that the *t-tests* results of the initial drafts and the final versions of Task A score analytically in content and language accuracy by human raters and total scores generated by EWS database to investigate whether the gain is significant.

Table 5.13 *t-tests* results of scores in Task A (Initial vs. Final)

Category	Mean of initial drafts	Mean of final versions	t-value	Significance
Content	74.60±1.47 (7.35)	79.58±1.06 (5.32)	−4.371	0.000*
Language	74.22±1.28 (6.38)	78.26±0.97 (4.86)	−4.444	0.000*
Total	71.72±2.10 (10.52)	77.10±0.89 (4.43)	−3.056	0.005*

Notes: The table shows the results of mean (± SE). The numbers in the parentheses are the standard deviation of each item. * represents significance and the significant effects (p<0.05).

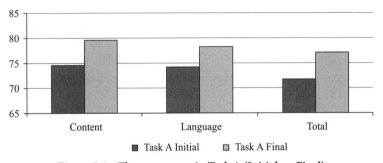

Figure 5.4 The meanscoresin Task A (Initial vs. Final)

There is a significant improvement in content, language accuracy and total score of Task A, as Table 5.15 and Figure 5.4 show. In terms of content, the participating students performed significantly better in the final versions (M=79.58, SD=5.32) than in the initial drafts (M=74.60, SD=7.35), t (24)=−4.371, p=0.000 (two-tailed). In terms of language, they also improved significantly from the initial drafts (M=74.22, SD=6.38) to the final versions (M=78.26, SD=4.86), t (24)=−4.444, p=0.000 (two-tailed). Moreover, the total scores of the final versions (M=77.10, SD=4.43) were significantly higher than in the initial drafts (M=71.72, SD=10.52), t (24)=−3.056, p=0.005 (two-tailed).

Table 5.14 *t-tests* results of EWS measurements in Task A (Initial vs. Final)

Category	Mean of initial drafts	Mean of final versions	t-value	Significance
Paper length	374.40±19.28 (96.41)	381.40±15.17 (75.87)	-0.0780	0.443
Sentence length	18.63±0.62 (3.11)	18.27±0.73 (3.66)	0.965	0.344
Total word	185.52±7.40 (37.02)	184.88±6.44 (32.22)	0.171	0.865
MF 1,000	144.68±5.13 (25.65)	146.40±4.56 (22.82)	-0.626	0.537
SMF	15.04±1.22 (6.11)	14.92±1.17 (5.83)	0.196	0.846
AWL	11.72±1.18 (5.91)	12.76±1.12 (5.62)	-2.463	0.021*
Remainder	14.08±1.29 (6.46)	10.80±1.08 (5.42)	4.845	0.000*
Repetition ratio	2.01±0.05 (0.25)	2.06±0.04 (0.21)	-3.315	0.003*
Word length	4.63±0.05 (0.27)	4.60±0.04 (0.19)	1.059	0.300

Note: The table shows the results of mean (± SE). The numbers in the parentheses are the standard deviation of each item. * represents significance and the significant effects ($p<0.05$).

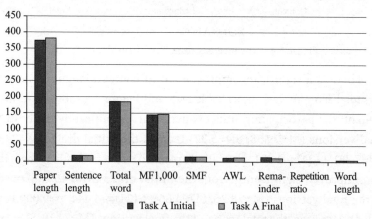

Figure 5.5 EWS measurements in Task A (Initial vs. Final)

With regard to the effects of the integrated feedback approach on Task A, the statistics in Table 5.14 and Figure 5.5 show that the participating students experience no significant change in paper length and sentence length [t (24)=-0.0780, *ns*; t (24)=0.965, *ns*]. But the academic words have increased one word on average from the initial drafts (M=11.72, SD=5.91) to the final versions (M=12.76, SD=5.62), t (24)=–2.463, p=0.021 (two-tailed), yet the remainder words decreased 3.28 words from the initial drafts (M=14.08, SD=6.46) to the final versions (M=10.80, SD=5.42), t (24)= 4.845, p=0.000 (two-tailed). The repetition ratio of words increased a little [M=2.01vs 2.06, t (24)=–3.315, p=0.003 (two-tailed)]. The other vocabulary usage such as total words [t (24)=0.171, *ns*], the most frequent thousand words of English [t (24)=–6.262, *ns*], the second most frequent thousand words of English [t (24)=0.196, *ns*], and word length [t (24)=1.059, *ns*] demonstrate no difference between the initial drafts and the final versions of Task A.

2. Task B

Table 5.15 and Figure 5.6 show that the *t-tests* results of the initial drafts and the final versions of Task B score analytically in content and language accuracy by human raters and total scores generated by EWS database to investigate whether the gain is significant.

Table 5.15 *t-tests* results of scores in Task B (Initial vs. Final)

Category	Mean of initial drafts	Mean of final versions	t-value	Significance
Content	78.82±1.19 (5.94)	78.92±0.98 (4.90)	–0.077	0.940
Language	77.42±1.04 (5.20)	78.59±0.97 (4.83)	–1.114	0.276
Total	75.14±1.57 (7.86)	81.10±0.82 (4.09)	–4.588	0.000*

Note: The table shows the results of mean (± SE). The numbers in the parentheses are the standard deviation of each item. * represents significance and the significant effects (p<0.05).

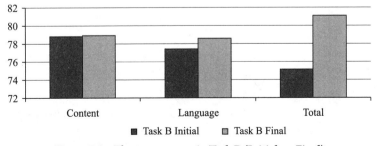

Figure 5.6 The mean scores in Task B (Initial vs. Final)

The integrated feedback approachs exerts no effects on Task B in both content [t (24)=-0.077, *ns*] and language [t (24)=-1.114, *ns*], as Table 5.15 and Figure 5.6 show. However, the total scores of the final versions in TaskB (M=81.10, SD=4.09) were much higher than that in the initial drafts (M=75.14, SD=7.86), t (24)=-4.588, p=0.000 (two-tailed).

Table 5.16 *t-tests* results of EWS measurements in Task B (Initial vs. Final)

Category	Mean of initial drafts	Mean of final versions	t-value	Significance
Paper length	361.72±19.92 (99.59)	410.68±22.15 (110.77)	–3.664	0.001*
Sentence length	18.66±0.82 (4.12)	19.05±0.87 (4.35)	–0.602	0.553
Total word	193.12±8.20 (40.98)	210.44±8.96 (44.79)	–2.875	0.008*
MF 1000	134.72±5.97 (29.84)	148.76±6.82 (34.11)	–3.955	0.001*
SMF	16.80±1.18 (5.89)	18.56±1.30 (6.52)	–1.745	0.094
AWL	10.72±0.81 (4.04)	11.68±0.80 (3.98)	–1.418	0.169
Remainder	30.88±1.93 (9.66)	31.44±1.79 (8.97)	–0.315	0.756
Repetition ratio	1.85±0.04 (0.20)	1.93±0.04 (0.20)	–3.781	0.001*
Word length	4.64±0.06 (0.29)	4.60±0.05 (0.27)	1.321	0.199

Note: The table shows the results of mean (± SE). The numbers in the parentheses are the standard deviation of each item. * represents significance and the significant effects (p<0.05).

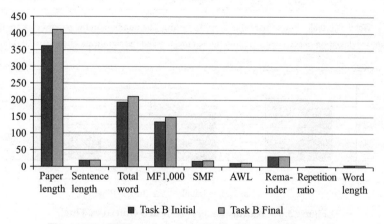

Figure 5.7 EWS measurements in Task B (Initial vs. Final)

With regard to the effects of the integrated feedback approach on Task B, the statistics in Table 5.16 and Figure 5.7 show that the paper length significantly increases in Task B. The participants produced on average 410.68 (SD=110.77) words in the final versions and 361.72 (SD=99.59) words in the initial drafts, t (24)=-3.664, p=0.001 (two-tailed). However, there is no significant change in sentence length [t (24)=-0.602, *ns*] after the use of the integrated feedback approach. In addition, participants significantly differed in the total number of words used between the two versions, producing on average 210.44 words (SD=44.79) in the final versions and 193.12 words (SD=40.98) in the initial drafts [t (24)=-2.875, p=0.008 (two-tailed)]. The most frequent thousand words also increased by more than 14 words, with an average of 148.76 (SD=34.11) for the final versions and 134.72 (SD=29.84), t (24)=-3.955, p=0.001 (two-tailed). Accordingly, the repetition ratio of word use also increased with an average of 1.85 (SD=0.20) in the initial drafts and 1.93 (SD=0.20) in the final versions, t (24)=-3.781, p=0.001 (two-tailed). However, the other vocabulary usage such as the secondary most frequent thousand words of English [t (24)=-1.745, *ns*], the academic words of English [t (24)=-1.418, *ns*], the remainder words which are not found on the other lists [t (24)=-0.315, *ns*] and word length [t (24)=1.321, *ns*] in Task B are not significantly changed.

3. Task C

Table 5.17 and Figure 5.8 show the *t-tests* results of the initial drafts and the final versions of Task C score analytically in content and language accuracy by human raters and total scores generated by EWS database to investigate whether the gain is significant.

Table 5.17 *t-tests* results of scores in Task C (Initial vs. Final)

Category	Mean of initial drafts	Mean of final versions	t-value	Significance
Content	79.00±1.22(6.12)	83.56±0.98(4.92)	−3.413	0.002*
Language	78.00±1.17(5.86)	81.08±0.82(4.10)	−2.803	0.010*
Total	73.40±1.94(9.71)	83.60±0.56(2.80)	−6.153	0.000*

Note: The table shows the results of mean (± SE). The numbers in the parentheses are the standard deviation of each item. * represents significance and the significant effects (p<0.05).

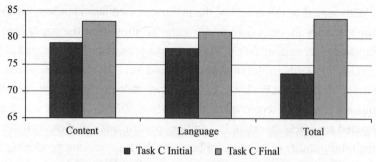

Figure 5.8 The mean scores in Task C (Initial vs. Final)

There is a significant improvement in content, language and total score of Task C, as Table 5.17 and Figure 5.8 show. The participating students significantly increased 4.56 points in content from the initial drafts (M=79.00, SD=6.12) to the final versions (M=83.56, SD=4.92), t (1,24)= –3.413, p=0.002 (two-tailed); and 3.08 points in language from the initial drafts (M=78.00, SD=5.86) to the final versions (M=81.08, SD=4.10), t (24)=–2.803, p=0.010 (two-tailed). There were also significant differences as a whole in Task C of the initial drafts and the final versions, and the scores of the final versions (M=83.60, SD=2.80) are about 10 points more than in the initial drafts (M=73.40, SD=9.71), [t (24)=–6.153, p=0.000 (two-tailed)].

Table 5.18 *t-tests* results of EWS measurements in Task C (Initial vs. Final)

Category	Mean of initial drafts	Mean of final versions	t-value	Significance
Paper length	345.24±20.11 (100.54)	389.36±22.69 (113.45)	–2.228	0.035*
Sentence length	15.86±0.71 (3.54)	16.32±0.72 (3.62)	–1.073	0.294
Total word	178.72±9.30 (46.51)	192.80±8.89 (44.46)	–1.824	0.081
MF 1,000	120.64±4.76 (23.80)	130.76±5.42 (27.09)	–1.930	0.066
SMF	15.16±1.39 (6.94)	18.04±1.65 (8.27)	–2.646	0.014*
AWL	12.44±1.61 (8.06)	13.84±1.67 (8.35)	–1.138	0.266
Remainder	30.48±3.79 (18.93)	30.16±3.72 (18.63)	0.273	0.787

(Continued)

Category	Mean of initial drafts	Mean of final versions	t-value	Significance
Repetition ratio	1.93±0.05 (0.25)	2.01±0.06 (0.28)	−2.099	0.047*
Word length	4.66 ±0.07 (0.36)	4.66±0.08 (0.38)	−0.075	0.941

Note: The table shows the results of mean (± SE). The numbers in the parentheses are the standard deviation of each item. * represents significance and the significant effects (p<0.05).

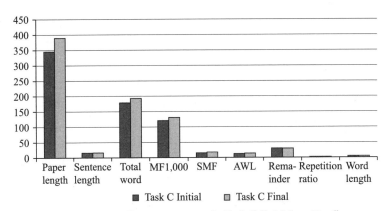

Figure 5.9 EWS measurements in Task C (Initial vs. Final)

With regard to the effects of the integrated feedback approach on Task C, the statistics in Table 5.18 and Figure 5.9 show that the average paper length of the final versions (M=389.36, SD=113.45) is 45.12 words more than that of the initial drafts (M=345.24, SD=100.54), t (24)=−2.228, p=0.035 (two-tailed). But the sentence length [t (24)=−1.073, ns] of the final versions demonstrated no significant difference from those of the initial drafts. Considering vocabulary choice, the participants significantly increased the use of the secondary most frequent thousand words of English, with an average of 18.04 (SD=8.27) in the final version and 15.16 (SD=6.94) in the initial version, t (24)=−2.646, p=0.014 (two-tailed). Meanwhile, the repetition ratio of words also significantly increased a little, with a mean of 2.01 (SD=0.28) in the final versions and 1.93 (SD=0.25) in the initial drafts, t (24)=−2.099, p=0.047 (two-tailed). There was no significant difference in the other vocabulary choice such as total words [t (24)=−1.824, ns], the most frequent thousand words of English [t (24)=-1.930, *ns*], the academic words of English [t (24)=-1.138, *ns*], the remainder words which are not found on the other lists [t (24)=-0.273, *ns*] and word length [t (24)=-0.075, *ns*] in Task C.

To sum up, there is a significant improvement in content, language and total score of Task A and Task C, while Task B shows no significant increase in content and language, but does have a significant increase in the total score.

4. The initial drafts of Tasks A, B and C

To across compare the three tasks, we ran the one-way ANOVA tests. The data in Table 5.19 and Figure 5.10 show that the participants write much longer sentences in Task A (M=18.63, SD=3.11) and Task B (M=18.66, SD=4.12) than in Task C (M=15.86, SD=3.54), $F_{(2, 24)}$=7.155, p=0.002 (two-tailed), but there is no significant difference in paper length in the three tasks in their initial drafts [$F_{(2, 24)}$=0.871, *ns*]. In addition, the participants used the most frequent thousand words of English in Task A (M=144.68, SD=25.65) than in Task B (M=134.72, SD=29.84), but least in Task C (M=120.64, SD=23.80), $F_{(2, 24)}$=5.174, p=0.008 (two-tailed). The remainder words which are not found on the other lists are also significantly different in the three tasks: they occur two times more in Task B (M=30.88, SD=9.66) and Task C (M=30.48, SD=18.93) than in Task A (M=14.08, SD=6.46), $F_{(2, 24)}$=20.946, p=0.000 (two-tailed). Meanwhile, the repetition rate of Task A (M=2.01, SD=0.25) was significantly higher than in Task B (M=1.85, SD=0.20) and Task C (M=1.93, SD=0.25), $F_{(2, 24)}$=5.066, p=0.010 (two-tailed). However, the results show no significant difference in other vocabulary use, such as the total word [$F_{(2,24)}$=1.288, *ns*], the secondary most frequent thousand words of English [$F_{(2, 24)}$=0.821, *ns*], the academic words of English [$F_{(2, 24)}$=0.482, *ns*] and word length [$F_{(2, 24)}$=0.083, *ns*].

Table 5.19 ANOVA results of EWS measurements (Tasks A, B, C in the initial drafts)

Category	Task A	Task B	Task C	f-value	Significance
Paper length	374.40±19.28a	361.72±19.92a	345.24±20.11a	0.871	0.425
Sentence length	18.63±0.62a	18.66±0.82a	15.86±0.71b	7.155	0.002*

(Continued)

Category	Task A	Task B	Task C	f-value	Significance
Total word	185.52±7.40a	193.12±8.20a	178.72±9.30a	1.288	0.285
MF 1,000	144.68±5.13a	134.72±29.84a	120.64±4.76b	7.689	0.001*
SMF	15.04±1.22	16.80±1.18	15.16±1.39	0.821	0.446
AWL	11.72±1.18	10.72±0.81	12.44±1.61	0.482	0.620
Remainder	14.08±1.30b	30.88±1.93a	30.48±3.79a	20.946	0.000*
Repetition ratio	2.01±0.05a	1.85±0.04b	1.93±0.05ab	5.066	0.010*
Word length	4.64±0.05a	4.64±0.06a	4.66±0.73a	0.083	0.920

Note: The table shows the results of mean (± SE). The numbers in the parentheses are the standard deviation of each item. * represents significance and the significant effects (p<0.05).

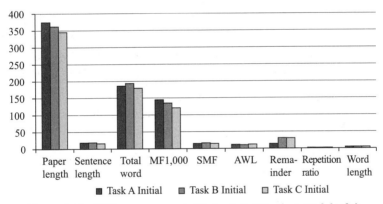

Figure 5.10   EWS measurements (Tasks A, B, C in the initial drafts)

5. The final versions of Tasks A, B and C

The difference of the items across the three tasks was further analyzed in the final versions with the one-way ANOVA test. The data in Table 5.20 and Figure 5.11 show that the participants write much longer sentences in Task A (M=18.27, SD=3.66) and Task B (M=19.05, SD=4.35) than in Task C (M=16.31, SD=3.62), F (2, 24)=5.134, p=0.010 (two-tailed), but there is no significant difference in paper length of the three tasks in their initial drafts [F (2, 24)=0.750, *ns*]. The total words of the final versions differ significantly across the three tasks. The participants use the most words (M=210.44, SD=47.99) in Task B, which is significantly higher than in Task A (M=184.88, SD=32.22), but not different from that in Task C (M=192.80, SD=44.46), F (2, 24)=3.928, p=0.026 (two-tailed). The most frequent thousand words of English in the final version also are significantly different across the three tasks, and the participants use much more such words in Task A (M=146.40, SD=32.22) and Task B (M=148.80, SD=34.11) than in Task C (M=130.76, SD=27.09), F (2,24)=4.166, p=0.021 (two-tailed). The secondary most frequent thousand words of English across the tasks also demonstrate the significant difference, and the participants use less of this type of word in Task A (M=14.92, SD=5.83) than in Task B (M=18.56, SD=6.52) and Task C (M=18.04, SD=8.27), F (2, 24)=4.208, p=0.028 (two-tailed). There is also a significant difference in the number of the remainder words which are not found on the other lists across the three tasks. The participants use almost three times more of these words in Task B (M=31.44, SD=8.97) and Task C (M=30.16, SD=18.63) than in Task A (M=10.80, SD=5.42), F (2, 24)=33.624, p=0.008 (two-tailed). In addition, the repetition rate of words in Task A (M=2.06, SD=0.21) was significantly higher than in Task B (M=1.93, SD=0.20), but was the same as in the Task C (M=2.01, SD=0.28), F (2, 24)=4.419, p=0.024 (two-tailed). However, there are no significant differences in the use of academic words [F (2, 24)=1.507, *ns*] and word length [F (2, 24)=0.464, *ns*] across the three tasks in the final versions.

Table 5.20 ANOVA results of EWS measurements (Tasks A, B, C in the final versions)

Category	Task A	Task B	Task C	f-value	Significance
Paper length	381.40±15.17a	410.68±22.15a	389.36±22.69a	0.750	0.478
Sentence length	18.27±0.73a	19.05±0.87a	16.31±0.72b	5.134	0.010*
Total word	184.88±6.44b	210.44±8.96a	192.80±8.89ab	3.928	0.026*
MF 1,000	146.40±4.56a	148.80±6.82a	130.76±5.42b	4.166	0.021*

(Continued)

Category	Task A	Task B	Task C	f-value	Significance
SMF	14.92±1.16b	18.56±1.30a	18.04±1.65ab	4.208	0.028*
AWL	12.76±1.12a	11.68±0.80a	13.84±1.67a	1.507	0.232
Remainder	10.80±1.08b	31.44±1.79a	30.16±3.73a	33.264	0.000*
Repetition ratio	2.06±0.04a	1.93±0.04b	2.01±0.06ab	4.419	0.024*
Word length	4.60±0.04a	4.60±0.06a	4.66±0.77a	0.464	0.631

Note: The table shows the results of mean (± SE). The numbers in the parentheses are the standard deviation of each item. * represents significance and the significant effects (p<0.05).

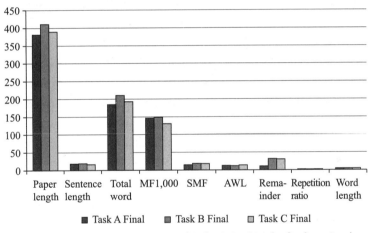

Figure 5.11 EWS measurements (Tasks A, B, C in the final versions)

Results showed a consistent improvement in students' performance from Task A through Task C both in initial drafts and final versions. It appears that the integrated feedback approach is relatively effective in helping students to improve their drafts through ongoing feedback, as it aims to sustain their writing development across tasks over time.

5.3 Summary

The analysis of students' writing performance resulted in four major findings.

First, the textual data analysis indicated that the integrated feedback approach played a significant role in supporting students' multi-drafting. They rewrote and revised six drafts on average for each task due to the training guided by the integrated feedback approach.

Second, the textual analysis suggested that the integrated feedback approach could launch revisions evenly in students' writing both in language accuracy (52%, n=455) and content (48%, n=425), although different feedback sources impact their writing development differ. More AWE feedback is incorporated than teacher feedback and peer feedback but the teacher and peer feedback appear to bring about a higher percentage of meaning-change revision while most AWE-influenced revisions happened at surface level. Students tend to make more discourse-related levels of revisions based on teacher feedback than the lexical and syntactic changes they tend to make based on peer feedback and AWE feedback. Students used teacher feedback mostly at the paragraph level with a good balance at the word level, syntactic level and mechanics level and the purpose of their revisions was more related to meaning deletion at meaning changes level and structure adjustment at surface change level. Students use AWE feedback at word and mechanic level and the purpose of revision is meaning clarification at word level and grammatical changes. Regarding peer feedback, students tend to use less comparing with other sources but the purpose of revision is more at surface changes than meaning changes.

Third, 70% (n=618) revisions were introduced by students with the help of AWE software and peer while 30% (n=262) revisions were elicited by teacher feedback. After receiving multi-sourced feedback, the individual writers themselves more often revised their papers at the syntactic level (41%) and paragraph level (45%) than the word (17%) and mechanic level (2%) and the purpose of their revisions was mostly concerned with elaboration of content ideas (36%) rather than surface changes (9%).

Fourth, results of *t-test* analysis and ANOVA of analytical and holistic human and machine scores of students' writings showed that there were significant differences between, within, and across tasks/drafts as well as between the pre-test and post-test.

The results of improved student performance suggested that the attempt at implementing the integrated feedback approach in the writing classroom was successful. Hence, the integrated feedback approach is effective in motivating learners to make substantial changes to their texts and consequently improve the quality of their writing.

Chapter 6
The Integrated Feedback Approach: Issues Within and Beyond

This chapter draws together what has been learned based on the impact of the integrated feedback approach on students' perceptions and performance in Chapter 4 and Chapter 5 in an attempt to explore the factors influencing the implementation of the integrated feedback approach and the potential issues identified from the study.

6.1 The integrated feedback approach: Process and product

The most important role of response is to help students to develop into independent writers who are able to critique and improve their own writing (Hyland & Hyland, 2006), so does the purpose of the implementation of the integrated feedback approach. According to the results of data analysis in Chapter 4 and Chapter 5, after experiencing the activating lecture, multiple-sourced feedback process and the feedback workshop, the individual writers' writing process and product witnessed changes in different degrees. This section discusses the contradictions and consistency between students' perceptions and performance in terms of their writing processes and products in order to probe how each stage of the integrated feedback approach co-function to affect students' learning to write in English.

6.1.1 Students' writing process

The purpose of the integrated feedback approach was to push

students toward increased responsibility, and ultimately independence, in the revision of drafts for linguistic correctness and content development. The data suggested that it did activate students' agency in revision performance by themselves through interaction with their instructor, their fellow students and the AWE program. In other words, the integrated feedback approach succeeded in creating a feedback-rich environment for individualized learning, with students solving their own difficulties in revision and instructors having fostered students' autonomy without total dependence on teachers.

Through the analysis of the impact on the students' perceptions, all the students preferred human feedback to machine feedback. The majority of students (n=23) favored teacher feedback to peer feedback or AWE feedback, while two students favored peer feedback rather than teacher feedback or AWE feedback. However, according to the results of the impact on the students' writing performance, students used most feedback (35%, n=308) introduced by AWE software, the second-most teacher feedback (30%, n=262), self-feedback (21%, n=191) the third, and peer feedback (14%, n=119) the least. There are contradictions obviously in students' perception of feedback engagement and performance, which is very interesting to be noticed.

According to the results of revision analysis in Chapter 6, AWE feedback and self-correction accounted for more than half of all the revisions (56%) students made in their final versions. The large percentage of changes assigned to students themselves is consistent with earlier studies by Paulus (1999), where 52% of the changes were stimulated not by peers or the instructor but some other source, including the individual writers themselves. On top of this, if the revision changes stimulated by peer feedback were added to the number of revisions introduced by AWE feedback and self-correction, more than two-thirds (70%) of the revision changes were made by students' decision, although most changes were at the lexical and syntactic levels. In these circumstances, automated writing evaluation and peer review could elicit two thirds of the revision changes. Consequently, teachers may spend less time commenting on students' language accuracy, allowing them to focus on other aspects of their teaching, and providing students with more extensive feedback in a much shorter turn-around time on contents.

After receiving feedback from different sources in different modes, the individual writers revised more often at the syntactic level (41%) and paragraph level (45%) than the word (17%) and mechanics level (2%): the purpose of their revisions was mostly concerned with meaning clarification, redundant meaning deletion, expansion and further elaboration of content ideas. Students themselves, it is argued, have a necessary role in taking responsibility for assessing their own work. Butler and Winne (1995) locate the giving of feedback within a model of self-regulated learning. They conclude that "monitoring is the hub of self-regulated task engagement and the internal feedback it generates is critical in shaping the evolving pattern of a learner's engagement with a task" (p. 275). In this study, students were activated to control their own learning by receiving and giving feedback to enhance their learning to write.

To further explore the factors affecting students' writing process, specifically, revision performance, the following four factors were identified. First, through the use of the AWE program, students could easily get feedback from the program whenever they needed it. They did not need to contact anybody and waited for the feedback after a certain period of time, as they had acknowledged the convenience and rapidity. Second, because of the existence of the peer response group, students were required to send their drafts after using AWE feedback to their peers. In order to impress their peers and gain their confirmations, students tried to revise their drafts more in language and content. Third, student revisions may also be affected by teacher feedback and the possibility of their written work being chosen as a sample piece. The teacher feedback was given in both written and recorded oral feedback in the Tripartite Evaluation Model by always highlighting the strengths of the paper, and then pointing out any weaknesses, eventually giving suggestions for revisions to the article. Last, student revisions may be entirely self-motivated: after they attended the activating lecture, they got a clear understanding of the task specification and assessment criteria, which was a good start to write an article; after they used AWE feedback they might revise other parts of the article accordingly; and after they obtained feedback from teacher and peer, they still might revise other parts of the article out of their own will; and as they practiced giving feedback to their peers in their group and attended the feedback workshop, their confidence in improving the quality of their writing was enhanced and their agency of control over their own texts were also boosted to a higher degree.

6.1.2　Students' writing product

Central to the rationale of the integrated feedback approach is to provide a mechanism through which the students could acquire and utilize evaluation skills to improve their learning to write. In contrast, it is a system where the evaluation of the process complements that of the product, where learning and assessment concur, and where learner independence is openly fostered. It should be able to guide the feedback practice of different feedback sources to collaboratively enhance students' learning how to write by emphasizing the active role the students play in their own learning.

Through the analysis of the impact on the students' perceptions, all the students' self-reported improvement in their writing over the semester at different degrees because of more interactions with the instructor, peer students and the AWE software, more and more practice with revision motivated by the integrated feedback approach. Meanwhile, results of *t-tests* analysis of analytical and holistic human and machine scores of students' writing products for the pre-test and post-test showed that there were significant differences, which indicated the students' improvement over the semester. Moreover, results of *t-tests* analysis and ANOVA of analytical and holistic human and machine scores of students' writing products showed that there were significant differences between drafts and across tasks, which indicated the students' improvement between drafts and across tasks. The results of improved student performance suggested that the attempt at implementing the integrated feedback approach in the writing classroom was partially effective. Hence, the integrated feedback approach is effective in improving the quality of their writing. Thus, there is obvious consistency in perception and performance of writing improvement because of the integrated feedback approach.

To further explore the factors affecting students' writing products, the following aspects were identified. Clear task-specific assessment criteria can be one: comparing to broad criteria, task-specific criteria can help students see the link between teaching and assessment and are more likely to give students a clear idea about how their writing performance relates specifically to the learning objectives pertaining to specific writing tasks. Group dynamics can be another: data revealed that group dynamics can strongly influence the implementation of the integrated feedback approach on the quality of the students' writing products.

6.1.3 The coordination and collaboration of different stages

The results of the data analysis in Chapter 4 and Chapter 5 do point to the potential of the integrated feedback approach to activate students to learn how to write through coordination and collaboration of its different stages and componential parts in the tertiary EFL writing classroom as shown in Figure 6.1.

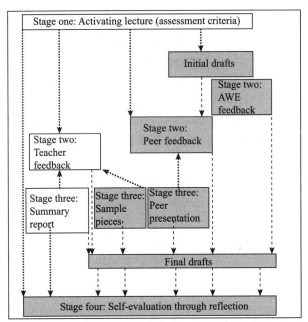

Figure 6.1 **The coordination and collaboration of different stages**

The most important process could be the self-evaluation through reflection, the fourth stage of the integrated feedback approach, which was designed to push students to reflect on gains as well as problems they had had in one assignment, and thus hopefully avoid repeating them in the next task. Through reflection, students can identify linguistic or organizational writing problems, or otherwise. All the componential parts and processes of the integrated feedback system hinge on students' internalization and reflection. If the students do not involve themselves in the different stages of the integrated feedback approach, then there is no use to have designed and practiced such a seemingly complicated feedback system in the framework of AFL. Students reflect on their strengths and weaknesses according to the external feedback they obtain from different sources and modes, while at the same time they could produce their own internal feedback on their own writings and incorporate them into their final versions in reference to the task-specific and course-related assessment criteria.

For students, among all the stages and processes of the integrated feedback approach, the core of the integrated feedback system might be the teacher feedback, which was designed to be the most important channel of extending classroom teaching to promote students' learning to write in English. It aimed to pinpoint students' strengths and weaknesses by referring to the genre features and assessment criteria that had been explicitly taught in the activating lecture of the approach (Stage one) and reinforced in the feedback workshop (Stage three) by the summary report and sample pieces. The activating lecture, the summary report and sample pieces are all connected to teacher feedback through the task-specific assessment criteria. Teacher feedback easily survives into students' final versions, both in content and language accuracy.

Then comes the peer feedback, which had the most potential and was the most dynamic process for students to learn how to write effectively from a social learning perspective. It is functioning in a double role as both input and output, which is closely related to the activating lecture of the approach (Stage one), the peer presentation and sample pieces (Stage three) with the assessment criteria. Some of the peer feedback but not all would be used critically in students' final versions to improve in a small way in content and most in language accuracy.

The process with the lowest impact may be the use of AWE feedback, which may survive to students' final versions directly and students might refer to it when they reflect on their writing problems. It is, however, independent from other processes if the instructor does not refer to it in classroom instruction in the third stage. Although students are not completely satisfied with the feedback points generated by the program, they used them for improvement in content scarcely but language accuracy substantially.

The feedback workshop (the third stage) is quite important to reinforce the function of different stages. The feedback points given in the study, besides AWE feedback, all centered the task-specific assessment criteria which were extensively used in the peer feedback and teacher feedback processes, and partially applied in the feedback workshop and the self-evaluation through reflection process. Comparing to broad criteria, task-specific criteria are more likely to give students a clear idea about how their writing performance relates specifically to the learning objectives pertaining to specific writing tasks. It is important for students to know the assessment criteria, and write and respond to them, but that can not guarantee the quality of the revisions. And it is very hard to measure the successfulness of revision changes.

6.2 The integrated feedback approach: Roles of participating parties

In order to overcome the limitations of the summative one-shot feedback approach, the integrated feedback approach presupposes the need to refocus feedback practice away from the notion of instructors providing one-way feedback to students in favor of dialogic exchanges in which instructors and students are jointly involved in conversations about learning (Beaumont et al., 2008). Then in such a case, what are the roles of the participating parties—the instructor, the students and the technology for the implementation of the integrated feedback approach? And what are the new roles that the integrated feedback approach enacted writing instructors and students in the writing classroom?

6.2.1　The instructor

For the implementation of the integrated feedback approach, the first participating party is the course instructor for it requires a heavy commitment and courage level on the part of the teacher. The instructor in this study has held a teaching position in the university for over 20 years, and has risen to the rank of full professor and PhD supervisor in the area of applied linguistics. She has a strong interest in teaching writing courses and research on writing pedagogy and assessment. Although she is also a very experienced language testing expert, she believes that assessment should be closely related to teaching and learning, which is the core concept of AFL. She is very experienced in teaching this course: since 2007 when the course series was listed as a national excellent course, she has been teaching this course for 12 semesters during 6 academic years. Generally speaking, her beliefs of teaching and assessment are quite open and she is ready not only to discuss them but also to reflect critically on them.

Anson (1989), for instance, has argued that the ways teachers judge writing and define their role when giving feedback are influenced by their belief systems. Such beliefs are partly the result of personal constructs but also originate from the social context in which teachers work. He suggests that teachers typically respond to student writing in one of the following three ways: dualistic responders focus largely on surface features and take the tone of a critical judge of standards; relativistic responders attend almost exclusively to ideational aspects of the writing, often ignoring significant linguistic and rhetorical problems; and reflective responders respond to both ideas and structure, and attempt not to be dictatorial in the approach. Developments in teaching theory and research have perhaps moved many teachers away from a dualistic response style, seeing it as prescriptive and potentially damaging to students' writing development.

Severino (1993) adds a socio-political dimension to this, pointing out that the nature of a teacher's response can suggest a stance towards both linguistic and cultural assimilation in L1 and L2 contexts. The researcher adopted Severino's point of view toward teacher response in this research.

In this study, the one-to-one teacher feedback was provided to the students in the Tripartite Evaluation Model proposed by Wang & Yang (2006). To adapt to the research purpose of this study, the researcher further modified it by adding a recorded oral feedback part, which facilitates students' writing and revising processes in the integrated feedback system. Students welcomed the combination and claimed a positive impact on their revision of drafts and even their main reason for continuing taking the course as detailed in the results of the data analysis of the impact on students' perceptions of learning to write in English in Chapter 5. Another piece of good news about the recorded oral feedback is that it can save a lot of the instructors' time in writing comments in English and it could be kept as a reminder to students to check what the instructor thought about the article and how did the instructor comment on it. When we gave feedback to the students, we discovered another function of recorded oral feedback: if a sample piece is chosen, the instructor could fully describe all the points that we hope the other students would pay more attention to in the sample pieces in recorded oral feedback. As it was an exciting and innovative endeavor in this study, students said they would listen to it many times and wrote of its personal value in their reflective journals. Thus, the recorded oral feedback also helped to build a good relationship between the teacher and the students.

The data of the study suggests that the function of teacher feedback in Tripartite Evaluation Modal is two folds in the integrated feedback approach: besides giving students concrete feedback to their work, it is also the model for students to give peer responses to their fellow classmates in the current study. By doing this, they could improve their evaluating ability and then improve their own writing ability. 23 (96%) students prefer written and recorded oral teacher feedback most, peer feedback second, and AWE feedback last. Students used written teacher feedback, which accounted for almost one-third of all the revision changes, mostly at the paragraph level with a good balance at the word level, syntactic level and mechanic level. The purpose of revision was more related to meaning deletion at meaning changes level and structure adjustment at surface change level. This echoes the findings reported in Shehadeh's (2011) and Yang's (2011) studies that it was important for instructors to assume a leadership role in promoting either collaborative writing or peer evaluation in the EFL writing classroom, given that the capacity of autonomous learning needed to be trained or supported through an interpersonal environment especially with sustained guidance of teachers (Benson, 2007; Littlewood, 1999). Thus, through examining the results of the teacher feedback influence on students' revision changes, the instructor is the most important participating party in the integrated feedback approach.

6.2.2 The student as peers

By drawing upon relevant theories in AFL literature and social learning theories, the current research examined an integrated feedback approach by situating it within a community of English writing. The writing instructor and the students formed a community of writing where the writing instructor was the core member, and learning writers were periphery members. In the process of moving from periphery members to core members, student writers and the instructor worked together within this community of writing and interacted with each other through feedback to help students become more capable of writing in English throughout the whole writing process rather than on a single written product, as in the case of the traditional summative approach to writing. Thus, peers have an important role in the learning of how to write motivated by the integrated feedback approach.

The conceptual rationale for peer feedback is that it enables students to take an active role in the management of their own learning. It is an element of self-regulated learning (Bulter & Winne, 1995) by which students monitor their work using internal and external feedback as reference. Peer feedback in this dissertation means a communication process through which learners enter into dialogues related to performance and standards (Liu & Carless, 2006). Assessment criteria can help students see the link between teaching and assessment. This is based on Vygotsky's (1978, 1986) concepts of the Zone of Proximal Development (ZPD) which strongly suggests the value of receiving support from more experienced peers in the feedback process. Peer response groups are also designed to help students to gain humanistic support from each other and to avoid students becoming isolated from their peers. The instructor believes that students could move from "peripheral participation" to "full participation" (Lave & Wenger, 1991: 37) through addressing feedback from different sources while writing and rewriting their articles.

Regarding peer feedback in this study, the fact that students infrequently adopted their peers' revisions is noteworthy. Students tended to use less peer feedback (14%) comparing with other sources (AWE feedback, 35%; teacher feedback, 30%; self-feedback, 21%) and the purpose of revision is more at surface changes than many changes. This finding echoed Connor & Asenavage's (1994) study, which claimed that peer feedback made only a marginal difference to student texts, finding only 5% of revision could be directly linked to peer comments. Mendoca & Johnson's (1994) study, for example, suggested that students were very selective about using peer comments in their revisions. Villamil & DeGurrero (1998: 491) explicitly state that "peer revision should be seen as an important complementary source of feedback in the ESL classroom".

Despite the predominant preference for teacher feedback, students felt that they could better internalize the features of good writing by judging and giving comments to their peers with reference to the assessment criteria. Such students' views correspond to the results of Lundstrom & Baker's (2009) study where they found the "giver" (reviewers) benefited more from peer evaluation and had more gains in their writing performance than the "receivers" (writers). Since student reviewers perceive that other students experience the same difficulties in writing that they do, peer feedback may also lead to a reduction in writer apprehension and help them to develop their autonomy and self-confidence as writers (Chaudron, 1984; Curtis, 2001; Coterall & Cohen,

2003). Peer response is seen as a way of giving more control and autonomy to students since it involves them actively in the feedback process as opposed to a passive reliance on teachers' feedback to "fix" their writing (Mendoca & Johnson, 1994). Freedman & Sperling (1985), Mittan (1989) and Caulk (1994) posit that peer response provides students with an audience for their writing which is more authentic than teacher response tends to be. It also enhances the ability of peer reviewers to evaluate their own work by providing a sense of audience and a checklist of evaluative questions to apply to their own writing (Cheng & Warren, 1996; Stoddard & MacArthur, 1993).

There appear to be two main issues in implementing peer feedback: the grouping of peers and the method of peer training. Data revealed that group dynamics can strongly influence the implementation of the integrated feedback approach on student learning to write. There are altogether 10 groups in the class, each having three members. Considering their group dynamics, there are three kinds of groups in the class: groups in which all three members of the team are very cooperative with each other; groups in which only two of the students can work really well with each other, or groups in which none of the three students is cooperative. Some of the groups were very poor at time management. Ma (2010) makes some interesting points about the importance of previous experience in understanding the factors that influence the decisions that students make when responding to their peers' writing, suggesting that training sessions may need to take into account students' previous learning experiences and especially their assessment experiences in high stakes tests.

Thus, as teachers, we need to consider students' goals of choosing the course, their self-reported English writing proficiency, their writing ability in their first task and their self-introduction about their personality and learning experience, as well as their schedule for the semester. So, it is a high priority to know the students in order to group them well before we implement the integrated feedback approach. Thus, at the beginning of the semester, in order to guarantee the implementation of the integrated feedback approach, teachers should collect students' information on reasons for selecting the course, expectations of the course, feedback preferences, and group division intentions and use the evaluative and diagnostic function of the first task of the course as a writing proficiency measurement.

Despite the success of the implementation of the integrated feedback approach, we were aware of a number of problems. Two evident flaws related to peer review are the inadequate use of the peer review forms, and the training of peer review. However, these can be remedied by training students more directly in feedback provision and feedback use strategies by adjusting the balance in marking scheme in order to better accommodate the process. In this study, students in one team need to be working together across different task types for a whole semester. The once-for-all training mode is far from enough in a real classroom situation; thus sustainable feedback training for peers is urgently needed to guarantee the smooth implementation of the integrated feedback approach. Peer review training in the first class was far from enough, and as a result, the students felt that their peers' comments usually lacked substantial suggestions, which may result in the less use of peer feedback. They not only need to be trained in the general skills of reviewing a paper, but they also need to be trained for the reviewing of a specific task with the assessment criteria assigned by the instructor. An additional point that should be made here is that the training is also likely to benefit student reviewers themselves as they are in a better position to view their own texts from a reader's perspective (Hyland, 2003; Ferris, 2004). This echoes Berg's (1999) and Stanley's (1992) recommendations that training should be given to all L2 writers. The students should have first received training and learned response rhetoric. The training could help students become effective responders and highlight areas that they needed to be concerned about when writing and responding. In this study, the peer review presentation actually is a kind of peer review training, using the presentation group as an example; however, the timing of it is a problem, which should have been put after the peer-review evaluation. Research by Stanley (1992) suggested that students who received training and coaching looked at their peers' writings more closely and offered more specific guidelines for revision than untrained students. Students who received training developed better quality responses, which contained more specific suggestions for improving an essay.

Her research was later confirmed by Catherin Berg (1999) and Trena Paulus (1999). Training students to create quality feedback resulted in a baseline or a template from which all students could expect to receive specific suggestions for revising papers instead of simply receiving vague comments and empty praise.

Therefore, it is recommended that training should occur through practice. We need to train students in the whole course of the teaching class. This should be written into the course objective and corresponding teaching and assessing activity should be designed accordingly, such as peer review activities through in-class guided discussions. For peer training in a classroom situation, instructors should include introduce and familiarize the students with the process approach to essay writing and with effective responding concepts. Students also should receive instructions about generating quality e-feedback responses as previous research suggested. Comments were to include critiques, suggestions, questions, statements, and advice, as well as the typical praise comments students include. Students need to be trained on how to create effective responses and offered chances of hand-on practice, face-to-face communication and negotiation with peers who received the feedback.

6.2.3　The technology

An effective integration of modern educational technology with English writing instruction has been a common concern of practitioners and researchers in the field of language teaching in the 21st century. It reaches everywhere and affects teachers' teaching and students' learning in the language teaching classroom. With the development of educational technology, the interaction between students and the instructor, and among students themselves was broadened into the virtual space; they interacted with each other through the Internet, and more importantly, students realized their individual learning with the help of technology. In this study, the impact of technology is manifested in three aspects: first, classroom management; second, the media of interaction between the instructor and student, and among students themselves; and third, ways of feedback provisions and feedback engagement. The instructor's workload of running the integrated feedback approach is largely reduced because of the technology. Seriously speaking, without technological support, the implementation of the integrated feedback approach is not possible.

The integrated feedback approach allows for the development of a more collaborative and participatory learning environment that is more suited to the learning of how to write than other feedback models, for it created a good environment for learning writing. In order to foster a relaxing learning atmosphere and meaningful interaction between the instructor and the students, a multi-media communication highway was built between the instructor and the students in the Happy English Writing course, which includes communication through the text written by the students and teacher, peer feedback in the Tripartite Evaluation Modal, face to face communication, communication through conversation over cell phones, communication online, and students' reflective journals. Among these, teacher feedback and peer feedback are the core part of the communication between students and the instructor to motivate students to learn how to write in English through the Tripartite Evaluation Model, which has provided an interactive platform for student composition mediation between instructors and students, and among peer students. By reading and evaluating students' writing pieces, the instructors can understand more about their students, who will not have the chance to reveal to their instructors under other circumstances. So the interaction between students and the instructor through the media of the text is carried out when the instructor writes out comments to their pieces with the Tripartite Evaluation Model and records the oral feedback. The other means are all secondary to this one, including AWE feedback.

Compared to human feedback, AWE feedback has its own advantages and disadvantages. The data provided by the Pigai system at least provided evidence that students were making use of feedback to move closer to work that meets the criteria the software uses to evaluate their writing. The criteria used by the software may be no better or worse than those provided by the instructor for specific tasks, but at least there is evidence of using the feedback and the criteria, whereas there is no such evidence in the case of summative feedback provided to them.

However, the system is not immune to errors: the general disagreement between the Pigai system holistic scores and the quality of students' writing should be used as just one piece of evidence about the quality of students' writing or it could be totally ignored. In this study, although the instructor did not refer to students' scores from the system, students could not help but keep them in mind, and as time went on they become more at peace with the scores generated by the system. As a result, human feedback is still necessary to redress the limitations of AWE feedback. Students suggested that some instructional help from the instructor is needed to explain some of the problems students came across while applying AWE feedback to their writing learning.

From a practical point of view, a study of a hybrid use of computer-based feedback and human feedback is a new research and practice trend in feedback research such as this one. If computer-based feedback is probably best used in conjunction with human feedback, the question then is how teachers should react to sharing feedback responsibility in such a hybrid situation, and what approaches would be most effective. Would it be preferable for teachers to rely on computer-based feedback for mechanical errors, leaving them to concentrate on the content and organization of drafts revised on the basis of feedback provided by computer? In this study, we have obtained information on students' views of the program and the effects of computer-generated response as part of the integrated feedback approach. The potential of automated essay evaluation and computer-mediated feedback for improving student writing and developing their independent writing skills need to be further explored. In particular, how students synthesize AWE feedback with human feedback to improve their writing.

Since there are likely to be many developments in such software in coming years, this will be a prime area of research related to feedback, as will further research on areas of computer feedback such as online social interaction and revision practice. Technology changes our conceptions of both instruction and L2 Literacy as teachers continue to integrate technology into their writing classrooms. In fact, many developers of automated feedback software insist that computer-generated feedback should only be considered a supplement to, rather than a substitute for, classroom instruction (Burstein & Marcu, 2003; Burstein et al., 2004).

In this study, AWE feedback is a necessary complement to teacher feedback and peer feedback. According to the results of the data analysis in Chapter 4, students complained the most about the quality of AWE feedback compared to human feedback (peer and teacher feedback). AWE feedback was more problematic than human feedback in students' eyes and always ranked lower when compared to peer and teacher feedback. Students thought AWE feedback was predetermined and thus formulaic, and unable to provide context-sensitive responses especially in the dimension of meaning as a human can. However, according to the results of the data analysis of students' writing performance in Chapter 5, students incorporated more AWE feedback than human feedback revisions in their final versions at the word and mechanics level, making up more than one-third of all the revision changes. This finding echoed Yang (2004) and Yeh & Yu (2004) that the automated feedback is useful only for the revision of formal aspects of writing but not for that of content development. Other research also reveal key issues concerning the implementation of AWE in the writing classroom (Chen & Cheng, 2008; Yang, 2004) including approval of the rapid speed and accuracy of feedback (Elliot & Mikulas, 2004; Yang, 2004) as well as disapproval of inadequate feedback on essay content and the possibility of assessing student writing based on essay length (Herrington, 2001). Thus, it can be claimed that the use of AWE feedback had a positive effect on the quality of students' writing, although students tended to express a preference for human feedback over AWE feedback in their perceptions.

6.2.4 Multiple roles of the instructor and the students

From the current research, the integrated feedback approach, on the one hand, provided learners with opportunities to negotiate and reconstruct meaning in their writing while interacting with different feedback providers including computer, peer, teacher and self; and on the other hand, it also provided learners with much more opportunities to be independent from the instructor in their writing learning process. Student improvement and involvement in learning were much higher than the traditional feedback approach because they know their teachers and peers cared about their writing improvement and the efforts they put in. The student's role is extremely active, and there is strong evidence to suggest that the integrated feedback approach was able to enhance their motivation and self-esteem in writing. Thus, the integrated feedback approach supposes an important change in the roles of teachers and students alike, with learning and collaboration taking over from teaching and subordination. The new roles of the students and teachers help to construct new types of relationships between them in addition to the traditional teacher-student relationship in teaching, learning and assessing. The integrated feedback approach provides writing teachers and student writers with a different relationship from the traditional teacher-student one-shot feedback scheme.

In the traditional summative feedback approach to writing, teachers and students are engaged in an unequal relationship, with the teacher having absolute authority over students' writing products and students only obeying teachers' directions and requirements passively for changes in their texts without knowing what kind of criteria or standards the teachers applied to judge their writing. The one-shot summative approach is what students encounter when writing single drafts.

However, by employing the integrated feedback approach, teachers and students are assuming different roles and maintaining totally different kinds of relationships. Teachers share the learning goals and assessment criteria with students, while students are treated as active agents, rather than limited to the role of the passive or inactive responder to feedback. They construct the terms and conditions of their own learning, responding to and adapting their writing and revision strategies over a period of time based on the feedback they receive from multiple sources in multiple modes as indicated in Table 6.1. Redrafting, self- and peer-evaluation are built into the writing process, and students are prepared to deal with subsequent drafts themselves, using the feedback from the task-specific assessment criteria from the teacher and self- and peer-feedback. Recognizing that students have agency and encouraging them to use and develop their own feedback strategies may help them exploit the potential of feedback and assist their development as independent writers.

Table 6.1   New relationships of teacher and student

No.	Stages	Multiple roles of teacher and student
1	The activating lecture	Traditional teacher and student relationship is formed in the writing classroom where the student is subordinate to the teacher.
2	The feedback process	The teacher is not subordinating students. Students receive feedback from multiple sources and give feedback to their peers.
3	The feedback workshop	Students and the teacher are co-teaching and co-learning.
4	The self-feedback through reflection	The teacher withdraws from the learning scene and leaves students to self-reflect, self-revise, and self-evaluate.

Collaboration among the instructor and the students is of paramount importance for the integrated feedback approach to be successful. The instructor must believe that students could move from "peripheral participation" to "full participation" (Lave & Wenger, 1991:37) through addressing feedback while writing and rewriting their articles. In this study, the instructor and the students played different roles and formed different layers of relationships during the different stages of the implementation of the integrated feedback approach. In the activating lecture (the first stage), the teacher acted as a writing lecturer, task specification writer, assessment criteria designer and user, and analyzer of sample pieces while students acted as listeners, writing learners, and assessment criteria learners. They formed a normal teacher and student relationship in the writing classroom. In the feedback process (the second stage), the teacher acted as a teammate, a helper, a reader, an interactive feedback giver, a writing critic, and a consultant while students were critical feedback users, multiple draft writers, and process writing experiencers. Teachers are not subordinating students at this stage of the approach. In the feedback workshop (the third stage), the instructor was a drama director, an audience, a learner, and a question master while students were presenters, questioners, audience, and readers of sample pieces. Students and teachers were co-teaching and co-learning in this process. In the self-evaluation through reflection (the fourth stage), the teacher withdrew from the learning scene and left the students to be self-reflectors, self-revisers, self-feedback givers and self-evaluators.

6.3 The integrated feedback approach: Issues and challenges

Based on the above discussion, the integrated feedback approach proposed by the researcher refers to a four-stage feedback system which emphasizes the active role that students play in their own learning in writing, feedback and rewriting processes with the help of different feedback providers and effective instructional support centered on the task-specific assessment criteria. It encourages a reflective, active response to integrated feedback from different sources and in different modes which can be effectively useful for raising students' awareness of genre-specific conventions, developing independent learning skills, and improving writing products. When the integrated feedback approach was put forward in Chapter 2, it was not known how student writers would think of it relating to their learning to write and to what extent the approach could be effective to influence students' EFL writing performance in the tertiary learning context.

The impact of the integrated feedback approach was positive if the aims of applying the integrated feedback approach in Chapter 2 were considered. The participating instructor in this study attempted to clarify the course objective and learning goals of each task for students by sharing assessment criteria and familiarizing them with the requirements of writing tasks through explicit instruction and effective instructional supportive strategies. Meanwhile, students played active roles in the learning process through being engaged in multiple revisions, peer evaluation, and self-evaluation on a regular basis.

Considering the first aim, through the integrated feedback approach, the limitations of a summative assessment approach through a one-shot feedback procedure was resolved. The more evident consequence of this was that given more time to reflect on the feedback provided by different feedback sources, students could write more sophisticated, much more clearly expressed and refined articles as shown in Chapter 5.

In relation to the second aim, satisfactory results were obtained during the multiple-draft process and in the quality of the final products. Students had been provided with a large amount of data on their performance, and with the task-specific assessment criteria, they were well aware of the gap between their current performance and the expected performance during the process of writing and rewriting a satisfactory final product through interaction with the AWE system, fellow students, the instructor and self.

The third aim of improving learner independence had also yielded positive results, since to a large extent students had been responsible for their own progress. The most tangible evidence for this claim has already been reviewed in the analysis of the impact on students' perceptions and performance. Students sought help less often for the instructor, and clearly controlled higher-level text skills much better.

Last, as was out of our expectation, reduction of the frustration generated by timed essay assessment had obviously been fulfilled for students. Not only had the overall quality of the texts risen considerably, but the close interaction between the instructor and the students encouraged an atmosphere of collaboration in the writing learning process. This gave students a sense of achievement, which in turn increased their confidence and willingness with respect to future writing tasks.

Based on the analytical research results in Chapter 4 and Chapter 5, it can be concluded that the integrated feedback processes for students are more effective if the feedback is:

(1) Helping students to become familiar with the gap between an actual and desired performance and to close the gap, and corrective in such a way in which learners are guided with reference to the specific assessment criteria related to the goals of writing instruction for each task under the ultimate objective of the course;

(2) Focused on the task, specific, detailed, clear, corrective in such a way that learners are guided to improve their writing and therefore, help to close the gap between their actual and the desired performance;

(3) Specific, providing insights into the desired behavior, and provided in a dialogue in which good and harmonious relations exist between receivers and providers;

(4) Task and/or goal-directed, focused on the learning process, specific, in time and frequent, positive, unbiased, non-judging, constructive, having many details and/or justifications, and encouraging dialogue.

In short, the impact of the integrated feedback approach on students' perceptions and performance might have raised more issues concerning feedback in EFL writing classrooms than it has provided any definite solutions. The first issue that emerged from the study is whether more feedback leads to effective revisions and how to measure the successfulness of each revision stimulated by each feedback point. From the data analysis, students revised six drafts on average before the final submission and twelve changes for each task on average. As far as the quantity of revision elicited by the integrated feedback approach is concerned, however, do more feedback and revisions necessarily lead to the production of high-quality writing? The second issue that emerged from the study is how to most effectively use technology in curricula. A more pressing question is not whether educational technology should be used but how it can be used to achieve more desirable learning outcomes while avoiding potential harms that may result from limitations inherent in the technology. Is it an assistant, master, or something else? The third issue that emerges from the study is whether we should emphasize a product-driven or process-driven curriculum, or both, in order to cultivate students' writing abilities. With the guidance of the integrated feedback approach, everybody registers for the course formed a community of practice to learn how to write. While learning different tasks different participating parties would become the core members. The fourth issue that emerges from the study is how students recognize the authority (teacher, peer, or AWE software database) in the community of practice in class. The fifth issue that emerges from the study is how to handle the varying levels of feedback engagement by individual students. In this study, AWE feedback, peer feedback and self-correction yielded useful results in how response might lead to greater independence, while revealing what aspects students can revise without help from their teacher. Do some areas seem more accessible to self-assessment and, if so, which areas are these? What is the role of feedback in holistic education?

6.4 Summary

This chapter first discussed the contradictions and consistency between students' perceptions and performance in terms of their writing processes and products in order to probe how each stage of the integrated feedback approach co-function to affect students' learning to write in English. And then the roles of participating parties of the integrated feedback approach (teacher, peer students, technology) was presented respectively in order to explore the multiple roles of the instructor and the students, and new types of relationship between them in teaching, learning and assessing influenced by the integrated feedback approach. At last, issues and challenges emerged from the study in an attempt to reveal the effectiveness of the integrated feedback on students' perceptions and performance in terms of its aims.

Chapter 7
The Integrated Feedback Approach: Nurturing Positive Classroom Culture

This study explored how the integrated feedback approach influenced students' perceptions and their writing performance. It made an interesting and thought-provoking contribution to research in feedback on writing in a tertiary EFL learning context in Mainland China and pointed the way forward for more social-cultural research which moved from short-term experimental feedback treatments to richer naturalistic investigations over a semester focusing on feedback within the whole context of learning, teaching and assessing. This helps to expand knowledge and understanding of how different modes and sources of feedback can best contribute collaboratively to the writing learning of the EFL learners involved in the study.

Our study also attempted to shed light on the potential of the integrated feedback approach for promoting EFL students' writing learning in higher education in Mainland China. As a consequence of the descriptive and explanatory study, some suggestions would be proposed for English students, teachers, teacher trainers and assessment researchers in the tertiary EFL writing learning context.

7.1 Suggestions to students

A key feature of the integrated feedback approach that differentiates it from everyday understandings of feedback is that students are promoted to a central and active role in their learning process. They are always actively involved in monitoring and regulating their own performance, both in relation to desired goals and in terms of the strategies used to reach these goals. For the integrated feedback approach exploited for AfL purpose to work, students need to familiarize themselves with the seemingly complicated procedures to realize the benefits of the integrated feedback approach for promoting their writing learning, as well as their role in the process.

Students first need a clear understanding of the requirements of the writing tasks and must be sufficiently prepared for writing. They need to understand the nature of different writing styles and text that leads them to the subsequent appreciation and knowledge that they will draw upon as they write. They need to be clear about the assessment criteria that they will need to engage with for each piece of writing that they do: criteria that may change with the nature of the task.

Second, they should have open minds to accept critically all kinds of feedback information to help them to improve their writing ability. They need to realize the benefits of each feedback process involved in the integrated feedback approach to monitor and regulate their own learning, both in relation to desired goals and in terms of the strategies used to reach these goals. The interaction between the teacher and student, student and student, teacher and text, student and text, self and text, and student and machine occurred multiple times throughout the course while students were learning to write in English under the guidance of the integrated feedback approach.

Third, they need to play active roles in the assessment process through acquiring an understanding of the broad picture of the integrated feedback approach—that is, a much broader, multi-faceted process approach, rather than the one-shot product approach that they likely have been exposed to since primary school. Active student participation and engagement are crucial if the language learning potential of the integrated feedback approach is to be exploited in tertiary contexts. If students played an active role in the learning process through being engaged in creating multiple drafts and participating in peer and self-evaluation on a regular basis, their learning potential will be greatly maximized.

7.2 Suggestions to teachers

Implementing the integrated feedback approach in the framework of AfL in classrooms is challenging (Hall & Burke, 2003; Torrance & Pryor, 2001). It requires a culture change in the classroom and expansive learning on the part of the teacher (Webb & Jones, 2009). This study highlights the specific challenges faced by Chinese EFL writing teachers attempting to implement an integrated feedback approach.

First, the study shows that the implementation of the integrated feedback approach in English writing in higher education context in Mainland China requires professional knowledge and skills on the part of the instructor. Teachers need to have a clear vision of what the integrated feedback approach in the framework of AFL entails, a vision that needs to be in line with the instructor's beliefs and instructional practices. Thus, teachers need to examine current practice, and changes in attitudes, all of which lead to changed practice.

Second, teachers should foster a better link between assessment, teaching and learning in the writing classroom with the help of assessment criteria for specific tasks and the course, and in particular focus on how they can better use feedback to promote teaching and learning. Teachers have to teach what they assess, help students develop a strong grasp of AFL in writing and their role in the process, and make process writing, self-evaluation and peer-evaluation an integral part of students' writing experience. They should clarify learning goals for students by sharing assessment criteria and familiarizing them with the requirements of writing tasks through explicit instruction. They need to design instructional materials, procedures and develop their own criteria for good classroom assessment practice.

Third, since feedback is a very important link between teaching and assessing, teachers need to consider ways of involving students more fully in the process of using feedback in order to enhance its potential benefits in promoting learning. Teachers should help students to develop practices and strategies of feedback use which will scaffold and engage them as they develop their own self-monitoring capabilities.

Fourth, data analysis in Chapter 4 and Chapter 5 pointed to the existence of individual differences in the way learners processed and made use of feedback from different feedback sources. Students vary considerably in what they want from computer-based feedback, teacher feedback and peer feedback and how they use self-assessment as a feedback source. Thus, teachers need to tailor their feedback to suit each student, considering his or her backgrounds, needs and preferences, as well as the relationship between teacher and student, and the ongoing dialogue between them.

7.3 Suggestions to teacher trainers

In order for the integrated feedback approach in the framework of AFL to work, it is imperative to take account of teachers' professional development in assessment (Xu & Liu, 2009), home in on the learners' contexts (Hamp-Lyons, 2003), support them in their understanding of AFL and their role in the process, and tackle the challenges of successful implementation of AFL in spite of school and systemic issues (Carless, 2011).

Teacher education is, therefore, necessary to enhance teachers' assessment and feedback literacy and to equip them with the necessary knowledge and skills about the integrated feedback approach. If we consider feedback as an important teaching and learning tool, teacher training programs and curriculum designers need to address feedback issues as part of their focus and offer training in this area by providing guidelines and a range of techniques for teachers to use in their classrooms. This is not to advocate a "one size fits all" system of feedback, but rather to suggest that novice teachers need to be made aware of the range of options they can use when providing feedback and the possible benefits offered by these. This means they may fail to consider alternative feedback techniques if they do not experience them themselves. Teachers need to become familiar with the range of feedback types available and select from them, where possible, not only practices that are effective in that moment but also those practices that foster student autonomy in the long term (through, for example, self-regulation and self-evaluation) rather than creating dependence on a teacher.

Teaching training programs could work to raise teacher awareness of the latest developments in computer-mediated feedback and the strengths and weaknesses of these systems, so that they understand the possible ways these can be combined with other sources to create an integrated and effective feedback system. Such programs could also make teachers more aware of the different feedback sources and modes of delivery available to them and the possible ways of combining them to make an effective support system.

Teacher trainers also need to help teachers generate practical and practitioner knowledge and empower them through classroom-based action research, so that they figure out their own effective ways to give feedback without necessarily transferring findings from previous research.

7.4 Suggestions to classroom assessment researchers

Due to significant changes in the traditional assessment roles of teachers and students, classroom assessment researchers should consider the theoretical guidance of assessment: AAL, AFL and AOF when they design classroom assessment frame to embody the integrated feedback approach. For just as teachers are no longer considered to be transmitters of knowledge but facilitators of student learning and the student is no longer considered to be a receiver but a constructor of knowledge, so too are they no longer expected to behave respectively in classroom assessment solely as the "one who checks" and the "one being checked".

Appendices

Appendix A: Scores of pre-course and post-course writing measures

Appendix A-1
Pre-course and post-course writing measure scores by human raters

S	Phase											
	Pre-course measure						Post-course measure					
	Rater 1			Rater 2			Rater 1			Rater 2		
	C	L	T	C	L	T	C	L	T	C	L	T
1	6	6	6	6	7	6	7	6	7	8	8	8
2	6	6	6	6	6	5	6	6	6	8	7	6
3	5	5	5	6	6	6	8	6	7	8	7	6
4	6	5	6	6	6	6	6	6	6	5	5	5
5	6	5	6	6	7	5	5	5	5	4	6	5
6	7	6	7	6	7	5	7	6	7	7	6	7
7	6	6	6	6	7	7	6	6	6	5	5	5
8	7	7	7	8	7	7	5	5	5	6	6	6
9	5	5	5	7	6	6	6	5	6	7	6	6
10	5	5	5	6	6	6	5	5	5	7	6	6
11	5	5	5	6	6	6	6	5	6	6	6	6
12	5	5	5	7	6	6	4	5	5	4	6	5
13	7	7	7	7	6	6	5	5	6	6	6	6
14	6	5	6	5	6	5	7	7	7	7	7	7

(Continued)

S	Phase										
	Pre-course measure						Post-course measure				
	Rater 1			Rater 2			Rater 1			Rater 2		
	C	L	T	C	L	T	C	L	T	C	L	T
15	5	5	5	5	5	5	5	5	5	5	6	5
16	6	6	6	6	6	6	7	6	7	7	6	6
17	4	4	4	4	4	4	5	5	5	6	5	5
18	5	5	5	6	6	5	6	6	6	7	7	6
19	9	8	9	8	8	8	8	8	8	7	7	7
20	5	5	5	6	6	6	6	6	5	7	7	7
21	4	4	4	4	5	4	3	4	4	4	4	4
22	6	6	6	6	8	6	5	6	5	7	7	6
23	5	5	5	4	5	4	4	5	5	5	5	5
24	6	6	6	6	6	6	5	6	5	6	6	6
25	7	7	7	6	6	6	6	7	6	7	7	6

Notes: C=content; L=language; T=total

Appendix A-2

Pre-course writing measure scores and other textual information by EWS database

S	Total score	Paper length	Word total	Word types	Word repetition rate	Average word length	Average sentence length
1	76.98	269	134	105-10-10-9	2.01	4.85	15.82
2	70.02	226	110	93-6-6-5	2.05	4.33	16.14
3	75.3	217	127	103-4-8-12	1.71	4.63	14.47

(Continued)

S	Total score	Paper length	Word total	Word types	Word repetition rate	Average word length	Average sentence length
4	67	291	133	108-6-5-14	2.19	4.31	11.64
5	85.65	228	126	102-5-13-6	1.81	4.77	22.8
6	73.57	240	118	100-10-4-4	2.03	4.47	18.46
7	71.91	321	133	109-12-6-6	2.41	4.24	17.83
8	77.19	306	164	138-12-6-8	1.87	4.41	16.11
9	80.4	176	103	80-10-7-6	1.71	4.99	17.6
10	77.67	260	145	108-22-4-11	1.79	4.48	17.33
11	78.49	234	137	106-12-11-8	1.71	4.54	14.63
12	73.3	210	112	92-7-8-5	1.88	4.33	17.5
13	74.77	377	176	144-18-8-6	2.14	4.24	13.96
14	76.3	213	116	89-6-6-15	1.84	5.03	15.21
15	66.56	185	99	84-9-3-3	1.87	4.3	12.33
16	79.44	235	131	106-11-7-7	1.79	4.4	21.36
17	77.47	132	80	63-8-4-5	1.65	4.61	22
18	75.36	207	123	95-13-7-8	1.68	4.34	15.92
19	85.41	305	166	122-13-16-15	1.84	4.91	17.94
20	82.53	229	129	97-14-11-7	1.78	4.77	16.36
21	74.28	129	83	70-5-4-4	1.55	4.25	18.43
22	88.41	326	175	123-21-17-14	1.86	4.56	20.38
23	85.95	143	94	72-8-8-6	1.52	5	20.43
24	76.65	308	148	125-12-9-2	2.08	4.72	13.39
25	80	186	123	96-13-7-7	1.51	4.47	16.91

Appendix A-3
Post-course writing measure scores and other textual information by EWS database

S	Total score	Paper length	Word total	Word types	Word repetition rate	Average word length	Average sentence length
1	76.26	329	167	127-18-11-11	1.97	4.67	13.16
2	71.64	250	110	88-11-4-7	2.27	4.81	19.23
3	73.64	276	133	100-15-8-10	2.08	4.69	17.25
4	63.96	251	121	98-5-4-14	2.07	4.29	11.41
5	76.29	182	101	77-12-4-8	1.8	5.07	18.2
6	74.1	303	131	105-10-3-13	2.31	4.62	23.31
7	74	376	155	120-13-7-15	2.43	4.39	19.79
8	75.61	330	158	122-14-9-13	2.09	4.77	15.71
9	80.1	304	163	113-14-10-26	1.87	4.91	16.89
10	77.01	357	173	126-18-8-21	2.06	4.57	16.23
11	74.82	279	137	100-11-14-12	2.04	4.66	16.41
12	77.81	235	143	114-14-8-7	1.64	4.8	14.69
13	78.72	297	159	122-18-8-11	1.87	4.57	18.56
14	79.28	304	166	129-17-6-14	1.83	4.73	16.89
15	69.11	261	129	98-9-5-17	2.02	4.64	14.5
16	73.61	308	150	121-9-8-12	2.05	4.42	17.11
17	72.19	251	126	91-14-7-14	1.99	4.24	19.31
18	78.44	277	148	113-13-10-12	1.87	4.5	21.31
19	83.79	269	144	94-13-16-21	1.87	5.01	22.42
20	86.99	251	140	89-17-18-16	1.79	5.03	20.92

(Continued)

S	Total score	Paper length	Word total	Word types	Word repetition rate	Average word length	Average sentence length
21	74.03	127	87	71-5-8-3	1.46	4.61	14.11
22	82.14	296	165	113-18-13-21	1.79	4.59	21.14
23	86.44	172	105	71-13-10-11	1.64	5.12	24.57
24	74.87	264	144	114-11-9-10	1.83	4.81	14.67
25	83.21	215	138	103-13-12-10	1.56	4.78	19.55

Appendix B: Scores of Tasks A, B, and C

Appendix B-1
Analytic scores of content and language of Task A by human raters

S	Phase							
	Initial drafts				Final versions			
	Rater 1		Rater 2		Rater 1		Rater 2	
	Content	Language	Content	Language	Content	Language	Content	Language
1	85	80	85	85	85	80	85	85
2	85	75	75	70	80	80	78	75
3	70	75	85	70	80	80	85	75
4	75	75	60	60	75	75	70	70
5	70	70	60	65	75	75	65	65
6	75	80	70	70	75	80	75	75
7	80	80	70	70	80	80	85	75
8	80	80	75	70	80	80	75	72
9	70	70	65	70	80	75	85	78
10	80	80	75	75	80	80	75	75
11	75	75	50	50	80	75	85	80
12	75	80	75	75	80	80	78	78
13	70	75	70	70	75	80	80	80
14	80	80	80	75	80	80	80	75
15	75	75	70	70	85	80	85	80
16	80	75	85	85	85	80	90	90
17	75	80	50	50	85	80	65	60
18	75	80	85	80	75	80	88	85
19	90	90	90	88	95	90	92	92
20	75	75	75	75	75	80	80	78
21	70	70	50	50	75	80	70	70
22	75	80	80	75	80	80	88	95
23	80	80	80	78	80	80	80	78
24	80	80	75	70	80	80	75	72
25	75	75	75	80	75	75	70	70

Appendix B-2
Scores and other textual information of Task A by EWS database (Initial drafts)

S	Total score	Paper length	Word total	Word types	Word repetition rate	Average word length	Average sentence length
1	78.44	333	185	145-16-9-15	1.8	5.07	14.48
2	71.71	332	145	116-10-7-12	2.29	4.53	22.13
3	75.79	411	205	156-18-8-23	2	4.72	16.44
4	72.26	319	162	138-11-8-5	1.97	4.48	15.95
5	79.11	201	111	84-7-14-6	1.81	4.74	22.33
6	71.08	358	158	131-10-8-9	2.27	4.64	17.05
7	69.77	588	204	159-17-11-17	2.88	4.4	16.33
8	76.27	394	195	162-9-8-16	2.02	4.52	20.74
9	79.9	248	151	119-17-6-9	1.64	4.73	20.67
10	73	349	165	129-14-10-12	2.12	4.48	18.37
11	75.47	314	173	137-11-11-14	1.82	4.55	16.53
12	75.75	396	208	171-10-11-16	1.9	4.4	16.5
13	77.3	599	272	207-32-12-21	2.2	4.35	17.11
14	77.42	358	186	145-17-7-17	1.92	4.77	17.9
15	65.66	308	148	118-13-3-14	2.08	4.02	13.39
16	78.18	393	188	141-15-18-14	2.09	4.74	17.86
17	75.95	281	156	134-8-4-10	1.8	4.36	21.62
18	78.9	481	238	186-21-12-19	2.02	4.46	20.91
19	84.51	483	244	163-25-25-31	1.98	5.05	19.32
20	88.04	396	220	155-19-27-19	1.8	5.27	17.22
21	76.02	263	139	113-5-17-4	1.89	4.72	15.47
22	80.65	494	226	173-21-15-17	2.19	4.45	27.44
23	83.47	316	180	140-15-14-11	1.76	4.82	22.57
24	75.05	381	177	152-14-9-2	2.15	4.52	18.14
25	83.8	364	202	143-21-19-19	1.8	4.89	19.16

Appendix B-3

Scores and other textual information of Task A by EWS database (Final versions)

S	Total score	Paper length	Word total	Word types	Word repetition rate	Average word length	Average sentence length
1	76.92	331	181	144-16-9-12	1.83	4.94	14.39
2	72.17	340	151	126-10-8-7	2.25	4.47	21.25
3	74.96	412	202	156-19-8-19	2.04	4.65	16.48
4	68.86	316	151	134-7-8-2	2.09	4.58	13.74
5	78.66	320	160	126-11-18-5	2	4.7	17.78
6	71.25	358	158	128-11-9-10	2.27	4.65	17.05
7	69.04	494	173	136-15-10-12	2.86	4.48	17.03
8	76.28	413	204	178-8-8-10	2.02	4.47	19.67
9	79.74	323	171	137-18-9-7	1.89	4.65	23.07
10	69.7	336	160	129-13-9-9	2.1	4.42	14.61
11	75.96	312	164	134-9-16-5	1.9	4.34	16.42
12	74.56	369	184	158-9-10-7	2.01	4.29	18.45
13	77.78	538	250	192-26-13-19	2.15	4.55	17.93
14	76.85	361	186	148-17-7-14	1.94	4.7	18.05
15	65.3	304	147	118-13-4-12	2.07	4.29	11.69
16	76.94	349	169	128-14-16-11	2.07	4.73	17.45
17	77.41	334	170	140-12-9-9	1.96	4.57	23.86
18	79.37	514	255	197-27-16-15	2.02	4.47	17.13
19	84.04	502	244	168-27-24-25	2.06	4.93	20.08
20	83.9	357	192	140-11-27-14	1.86	5.04	16.23

(Continued)

S	Total score	Paper length	Word total	Word types	Word repetition rate	Average word length	Average sentence length
21	73.67	324	153	120-9-16-8	2.12	4.62	16.2
22	82.62	528	241	184-22-17-18	2.19	4.48	29.33
23	82.76	314	174	136-15-14-9	1.8	4.79	22.43
24	77.7	436	202	170-15-14-3	2.16	4.53	18.96
25	81.21	350	180	133-19-20-8	1.94	4.67	17.5

Appendix B-4

Analytic scores of content and language of Task B by human raters

S	Phase							
	Initial drafts				Final versions			
	Rater 1		Rater 2		Rater 1		Rater 2	
	Content	Language	Content	Language	Content	Language	Content	Language
1	85	80	85	85	85	80	85	85
2	85	75	75	70	80	80	78	75
3	70	75	85	70	80	80	85	75
4	75	75	60	60	75	75	70	70
5	70	70	60	65	75	75	65	65
6	75	80	70	70	75	80	75	75
7	80	80	70	70	80	80	85	75
8	80	80	75	70	80	80	75	72
9	70	70	65	70	80	75	85	78
10	80	80	75	75	80	80	75	75
11	75	75	50	50	80	75	85	80

(Continued)

S	Phase							
	Initial drafts				Final versions			
	Rater 1		Rater 2		Rater 1		Rater 2	
	Content	Language	Content	Language	Content	Language	Content	Language
12	75	80	75	75	80	80	78	78
13	70	75	70	70	75	80	80	80
14	80	80	80	75	80	80	80	75
15	75	75	70	70	85	80	85	80
16	80	75	85	85	85	80	90	90
17	75	80	50	50	85	80	65	60
18	75	80	85	80	75	80	88	85
19	90	90	90	88	95	90	92	92
20	75	75	75	75	75	80	80	78
21	70	70	50	50	75	80	70	70
22	75	80	80	75	80	80	88	95
23	80	80	80	78	80	80	80	78
24	80	80	75	70	80	80	75	72
25	75	75	75	80	75	75	70	70

Appendix B-5

Scores and other textual information of Task B by EWS database (Initial drafts)

S	Total score	Paper length	Word total	Word types	Word repetition rate	Average word length	Average sentence length
1	72.69	290	168	104-20-11-33	1.73	4.93	13.18
2	69.23	399	175	123-21-6-25	2.28	4.33	17.35

(Continued)

S	Total score	Paper length	Word total	Word types	Word repetition rate	Average word length	Average sentence length
3	80.07	271	165	115-11-9-30	1.64	5.37	19.36
4	73.84	304	175	127-21-4-23	1.74	4.15	20.27
5	73.53	515	235	167-21-14-33	2.19	4.37	17.17
6	74.39	455	203	140-15-14-34	2.24	4.6	22.75
7	72.51	406	200	154-15-7-24	2.03	4.3	17.65
8	74.03	308	172	122-13-9-28	1.79	4.3	22
9	80.28	284	175	135-11-5-24	1.62	4.63	31.56
10	71.62	260	143	106-13-6-18	1.82	4.55	18.57
11	71.72	282	171	124-10-8-29	1.65	4.44	14.84
12	79.34	442	221	142-17-16-46	2	5.17	21.05
13	79.77	506	278	202-31-13-32	1.82	4.47	18.74
14	72.29	382	203	143-14-4-42	1.88	4.58	15.92
15	76.86	275	155	107-15-14-19	1.77	5.06	14.47
16	75.57	472	249	183-15-17-34	1.9	4.56	16.28
17	72.1	236	148	99-12-8-29	1.59	4.6	15.73
18	78.43	300	169	129-16-11-13	1.78	4.63	20
19	77.11	388	196	118-19-12-47	1.98	4.96	21.56
20	74.82	338	183	120-14-11-38	1.85	4.67	19.88
21	72.08	263	156	107-16-12-21	1.69	4.46	13.15
22	71.8	432	215	157-18-12-28	2.01	4.43	14.4
23	79.63	199	136	85-11-13-27	1.46	4.89	22.11
24	82.02	549	287	181-35-19-52	1.91	4.79	23.87
25	73.8	487	250	178-16-13-43	1.95	4.7	14.76

Appendix B-6
Scores and other textual information of Task B by EWS database (Final versions)

S	Total score	Paper length	Word total	Word types	Word repetition rate	Average word length	Average sentence length
1	74.41	325	182	124-21-12-25	1.79	4.69	14.13
2	73.86	525	224	160-25-13-26	2.34	4.27	17.5
3	79.79	297	181	128-11-9-33	1.64	5.3	17.47
4	72.59	354	185	136-20-6-23	1.91	4.12	18.63
5	74.62	597	267	192-21-16-38	2.24	4.36	18.09
6	73.7	404	186	126-13-11-36	2.17	4.61	23.76
7	71.79	382	191	141-12-6-32	2	4.43	17.36
8	75.41	386	205	154-17-9-25	1.88	4.36	20.32
9	79.8	299	176	137-11-5-23	1.7	4.6	33.22
10	72.13	426	191	142-18-10-21	2.23	4.36	17.04
11	77.03	307	179	127-16-11-25	1.72	4.72	18.06
12	78.26	469	222	150-18-16-38	2.11	4.95	22.33
13	80.27	703	347	255-40-14-38	2.03	4.44	19
14	73.24	392	199	149-13-5-32	1.97	4.52	17.82
15	76.65	300	160	110-17-15-18	1.88	4.92	15
16	75.16	505	261	191-15-17-38	1.93	4.57	16.29
17	70.08	365	199	134-18-11-36	1.83	4.38	12.59
18	79.38	334	184	139-19-12-14	1.82	4.54	20.88
19	77.98	390	200	122-19-13-46	1.95	5.06	20.53
20	77.75	433	214	131-18-19-46	2.02	4.7	25.47
21	72.94	345	198	135-17-12-34	1.74	4.5	14.38
22	82.01	566	296	195-33-19-49	1.91	4.75	23.58

(Continued)

S	Total score	Paper length	Word total	Word types	Word repetition rate	Average word length	Average sentence length
23	78.11	209	142	91-12-11-28	1.47	4.84	20.9
24	73	453	221	163-21-12-25	2.05	4.36	15.1
25	74.15	501	251	187-19-8-37	2	4.53	16.7

Appendix B-7

Analytic scores of content and language of Task C by human raters

S	Phase							
	Initial drafts				Final versions			
	Rater 1		Rater 2		Rater 1		Rater 2	
	content	language	content	language	content	language	content	language
1	75	80	70	70	80	80	72	72
2	80	75	75	72	90	80	78	72
3	90	85	85	85	90	85	90	85
4	80	80	70	70	80	80	75	72
5	85	85	80	75	85	85	85	78
6	80	80	78	78	80	80	80	78
7	85	85	75	75	85	85	75	75
8	85	80	80	78	90	85	88	85
9	85	80	75	65	85	80	85	75
10	80	80	70	70	85	85	78	75
11	80	80	70	70	85	80	85	80
12	80	85	70	70	80	85	72	70
13	80	80	80	80	80	80	90	85
14	85	75	85	85	85	80	88	88
15	70	80	70	75	85	85	78	75

(Continued)

S	Phase							
	Initial drafts				Final versions			
	Rater 1		Rater 2		Rater 1		Rater 2	
	content	language	content	language	content	language	content	language
16	85	80	75	75	90	85	85	80
17	75	75	70	70	80	80	85	78
18	85	85	80	78	85	85	80	80
19	90	90	85	85	90	90	88	88
20	85	75	80	78	90	85	90	88
21	75	70	50	50	75	70	70	60
22	85	85	88	82	85	85	88	82
23	80	80	70	70	80	80	75	75
24	85	85	75	70	85	85	75	72
25	80	75	90	85	85	80	95	92

Appendix B-8

Scores and other textual information of Task C by EWS database (Initial drafts)

S	Total score	Paper length	Word total	Word types	Word repetition rate	Average word length	Average sentence length
1	68.55	310	159	96-29-4-30	1.95	4.44	11.48
2	69.32	488	172	132-14-5-21	2.84	4.06	19.52
3	75.52	407	230	135-30-11-54	1.77	4.54	12.33
4	63.78	219	115	89-13-1-12	1.9	4.19	10.95
5	72.78	336	155	111-11-9-24	2.17	5.08	14.61
6	71.2	228	124	97-7-8-12	1.84	4.57	14.25
7	73.35	373	180	119-10-18-33	2.07	4.78	13.32
8	74.51	366	179	142-16-5-16	2.04	4.47	17.43

(Continued)

S	Total score	Paper length	Word total	Word types	Word repetition rate	Average word length	Average sentence length
9	76.17	348	186	129-17-11-29	1.87	4.5	17.4
10	69.18	247	136	95-15-4-22	1.82	4.36	13
11	83.14	307	177	119-13-16-29	1.73	5.11	19.19
12	72.66	368	198	101-17-19-61	1.86	4.34	13.14
13	84.13	377	207	149-21-20-17	1.82	4.6	19.84
14	70.74	307	135	103-12-9-11	2.27	4.71	13.95
15	64.98	251	135	89-6-5-35	1.86	4.28	10.91
16	74.55	551	250	162-21-16-51	2.2	4.66	14.13
17	74.97	216	122	95-7-8-12	1.77	4.81	16.62
18	70.65	239	131	98-7-8-18	1.82	4.12	15.93
19	87.23	612	305	148-30-36-91	2.01	5.28	25.5
20	81.32	331	186	137-12-14-23	1.78	5.01	17.42
21	69.49	239	132	103-7-8-14	1.81	4.38	12.58
22	83.07	334	192	113-15-15-49	1.74	5.17	20.88
23	87.32	350	214	148-14-24-28	1.64	4.93	18.42
24	85.74	433	230	163-15-25-27	1.88	5.37	18.04
25	78.19	394	218	143-20-12-43	1.81	4.72	15.76

Appendix B-9

Scores and other textual information of Task C by EWS database (Final versions)

S	Total score	Paper length	Word total	Word types	Word repetition rate	Average word length	Average sentence length
1	69.64	321	167	99-31-5-32	1.92	4.34	11.89
2	69.09	525	180	140-15-6-19	2.92	4.02	18.1

(Continued)

S	Total score	Paper length	Word total	Word types	Word repetition rate	Average word length	Average sentence length
3	77.19	458	248	145-37-12-54	1.85	4.44	14.77
4	70.02	306	159	111-22-4-22	1.92	4.42	12.75
5	72.18	350	160	116-12-9-23	2.19	5.01	14
6	77.34	335	178	133-11-13-21	1.88	4.65	17.63
7	73.4	429	200	140-10-18-32	2.14	4.72	13.41
8	77.37	479	219	183-21-8-7	2.19	4.25	18.42
9	78.63	349	195	127-20-13-35	1.79	4.74	16.62
10	76.48	375	192	137-31-5-19	1.95	4.43	15.63
11	84.08	337	192	131-15-18-28	1.76	5.04	19.82
12	73.38	373	202	102-19-20-61	1.85	4.36	13.32
13	83.88	415	225	160-24-21-20	1.84	4.63	18.86
14	71.28	309	138	107-12-9-10	2.24	4.69	14.05
15	64.93	266	141	91-6-6-38	1.89	4.19	11.08
16	73.29	511	225	149-18-18-40	2.27	4.5	14.19
17	74.95	213	121	94-6-9-12	1.76	4.86	15.21
18	83.79	442	223	172-22-18-11	1.98	4.37	23.26
19	87.35	615	306	150-30-36-90	2.01	5.28	25.63
20	82.75	704	285	191-24-36-34	2.47	4.85	17.17
21	68.72	312	157	116-12-10-19	1.99	4.17	12
22	82.21	330	185	109-14-15-47	1.78	5.22	20.63
23	72.18	350	160	116-12-9-23	2.19	5.01	14
24	88.04	237	146	107-8-16-15	1.62	5.58	19.75
25	78.13	393	216	143-19-12-42	1.82	4.76	15.72

Appendix C: The assessing criteria for content and language

The assessing criteria for content and language

Score range	Description	
	Contents	Language
75–100	• The writing displays an ability to communicate with few or no difficulties for the reader. • The writing displays a logical organizational structure that enables the message to be followed easily. • Each paragraph has a single purpose and sub-topic. • Ideas flow smoothly and there is an effective use of transition markers to link ideas both within and between paragraphs. • The writing represents a relevant and adequate answer to the task set with adequate detail to support the points being made.	• Uses a wide range of vocabulary fluently and flexibly to convey meanings. • Produces rare errors in spelling and word formation. • Uses a wide range of structures with flexibility and accuracy. • Most sentences are error-free.
50–75	• The writing displays an ability to communicate although there is an occasional strain for the reader. • The writing is organized well enough for the message to be followed throughout. • One or two of the paragraphs may have mixed purposes or sub-topics. • The ideas generally flow fairly smoothly, but sometimes transition markers are lacking or inappropriate. • For the most part answers the task set, though some irrelevance and inadequate coverage of the task may be apparent.	• Uses an adequate range of vocabulary for the task. • Attempts to use less common vocabulary but with some inaccuracy. • Uses a mix of simple and complex sentence forms. • Makes some errors in grammar and punctuation but they rarely reduce communication.

(Continued)

Score range	Description	
	Contents	Language
25–50	• The writing displays a limited ability to communicate that puts strain on the reader throughout. • The writing lacks a clear organizational structure and the message is difficult to follow. • Most paragraphs have mixed purposes or sub-topics and paragraph boundaries may be inappropriate or lacking. • The idea only occasionally builds on one another and few, if any, appropriate transition markers are used. The writing is frequently irrelevant to the task set and only partially covers the task.	• Uses a limited range of vocabulary, which may be inappropriate for the task. • May make noticeable errors in spelling and word formation.
1–25	• The writing displays little or no ability to communicate. • Little or no organizational structure or message is recognizable. • The paragraphs have no obvious purpose and paragraph boundaries are apparently arbitrarily decided, if present at all. The ideas almost never build on one another and appropriate transition markers are not used. • The writing bears almost no relation to the task set and represents a totally inadequate answer.	• Uses only a very limited range of words and expressions with very limited control of word formation and spelling. • Use sentence forms but errors in grammar and punctuation predominate.

Appendix D: The end-of-course questionnaire

Appendix D-1

多元反馈形式的学生体验问卷（终稿）

同学，你好！本问卷为"多元反馈形式对学生影响力研究"的一部分，旨在调查"快乐英语写作"课堂上多元反馈形式的学生体验。所有问题均无标准答案，请仔细阅读并按要求回答下列问题，回答过程中请注意不要漏答。你的反馈我们将仅用于学术研究，但不会影响你的期末成绩。谢谢你的合作！（共 3 页）

2012 年 12 月

性别：□男　　　　　□女

专业：□文科　□理科　　　　□工科

学习英语的年限：_____ 年　联系方式：_____

本学期还同时上其他英语课吗？：□是　　　　　□否

目前英语水平：□已达到大学英语四级或相当水平

　　　　　　　□已达到大学英语六级或相当水平

　　　　　　　□已通过水平 1 考试

　　　　　　　□大学英语六级以上

一、单项选择题

		非常不同意	不同意	不确定	同意	非常同意
1	我很喜欢学习英语写作	1	2	3	4	5
2	我希望能够写出语言很流畅的英语作文	1	2	3	4	5
3	我希望能够写出没有语言错误的英语作文	1	2	3	4	5
4	英语"听说读写"四种技能中，我认为写作是最难的	1	2	3	4	5

（续表）

		非常不同意	不同意	不确定	同意	非常同意
5	我对快乐英语写作课"单周写作，双周评议，期间多元反馈，最后自评"的评价模式很喜欢	1	2	3	4	5
6	16周的英语写作训练后，我很有成就感	1	2	3	4	5
7	快乐写作课堂上的多元反馈形式很有效	1	2	3	4	5
8	反馈是提高写作能力的重要途径	1	2	3	4	5
9	修改对于提高英语写作水平很重要	1	2	3	4	5
10	反馈的形式越多，对英语写作水平的提高越有效	1	2	3	4	5
11	反馈点的数量越多，对英语写作水平提高越有效	1	2	3	4	5
12	反馈的内容越多，对英语写作水平提高越有效	1	2	3	4	5
13	修改的次数越多，写作的质量越高	1	2	3	4	5
14	我认为批改网对我的写作提高很有帮助	1	2	3	4	5
15	批改网很便捷	1	2	3	4	5
16	批改网评分及反馈很准确	1	2	3	4	5
17	批改网评分及反馈很可信	1	2	3	4	5
18	我对批改网关于篇章布局的反馈满意	1	2	3	4	5
19	我对批改网关于内容的反馈满意	1	2	3	4	5

（续表）

		非常不同意	不同意	不确定	同意	非常同意
20	我对批改网关于词汇的反馈满意	1	2	3	4	5
21	我对批改网关于语法的反馈满意	1	2	3	4	5
22	我对批改网关于标点符号的反馈满意	1	2	3	4	5
23	我对批改网关于作文主题的反馈满意	1	2	3	4	5
24	我会仔细看批改网的点评并对作文进行修改	1	2	3	4	5
25	最好在课堂上讨论一下批改网的点评内容	1	2	3	4	5
26	反馈有助于同学之间互相学习	1	2	3	4	5
27	同学互评需要适当培训	1	2	3	4	5
28	我认为同伴反馈对我的写作有帮助	1	2	3	4	5
29	同伴对我文章的正面评价增强了我的英语写作信心	1	2	3	4	5
30	我对同伴反馈很信任	1	2	3	4	5
31	我很喜欢同伴反馈	1	2	3	4	5
32	同伴反馈很及时	1	2	3	4	5
33	我对同伴关于篇章布局的反馈满意	1	2	3	4	5
34	我对同伴关于内容的反馈满意	1	2	3	4	5
35	我对同伴关于词汇的反馈满意	1	2	3	4	5

（续表）

		非常不同意	不同意	不确定	同意	非常同意
36	我对同伴关于语法的反馈满意	1	2	3	4	5
37	我对同伴关于作文主题的反馈满意	1	2	3	4	5
38	我对同伴关于标点符号的反馈满意	1	2	3	4	5
39	我会仔细看同伴的修改建议并对作文进行修改	1	2	3	4	5
40	我对助教关于篇章布局的书面反馈满意	1	2	3	4	5
41	我对助教关于篇章布局的录音反馈满意	1	2	3	4	5
42	我对助教关于内容的反馈满意	1	2	3	4	5
43	我对助教关于词汇的反馈满意	1	2	3	4	5
44	我对助教关于语法的反馈满意	1	2	3	4	5
45	我对助教关于作文主题的反馈满意	1	2	3	4	5
46	我对助教关于标点符号的反馈满意	1	2	3	4	5
47	我会仔细看助教的修改建议并对作文进行修改	1	2	3	4	5
48	助教的书面一对一反馈对我的英语写作提高很有帮助	1	2	3	4	5
49	助教的口头录音反馈对我的英语写作提高很有帮助	1	2	3	4	5

（续表）

		非常不同意	不同意	不确定	同意	非常同意
50	助教对我的肯定和鼓励增强了我的英语写作信心	1	2	3	4	5
51	课堂总体反馈对我英语写作提高很有帮助	1	2	3	4	5
52	课堂反馈中的小组评议展示对我英语写作提高有帮助	1	2	3	4	5
53	课堂反馈中的同学范文对我英语写作提高有帮助	1	2	3	4	5
54	自评反思过程使我能更好地消化多种多样的反馈	1	2	3	4	5
55	自评反思过程使我能够更好地认识到自己写作方面的长处和不足	1	2	3	4	5
56	快乐写作课堂上的多元反馈形式没有多少效果	1	2	3	4	5
57	16周的英语写作训练后，我对英语写作不再恐惧	1	2	3	4	5
58	16周的英语写作训练后，我的自我评价能力明显增强	1	2	3	4	5
59	16周的英语写作训练后，我的整体文章结构有了明显提高	1	2	3	4	5
60	通过16周的英语写作训练后，我的英语写作能力有了明显提高	1	2	3	4	5

二、多项选择题

我对不同反馈形式采用的回应方式表现在，可多选：

（　）1. 对于批改网的点评，我会在_____方面进行修改。

A. 语法　　B. 词汇　　C. 作文主题　　D. 标点符号　　E. 篇章结构

（　）2. 对于同学的反馈，我会在_____方面进行修改。

A. 语法　　B. 词汇　　C. 作文主题　　D. 标点符号　　E. 篇章结构

（　）3. 对于助教一对一的书面反馈，我会在_____方面进行修改。

A. 语法　　B. 词汇　　C. 作文主题　　D. 标点符号　　E. 篇章结构

（　）4. 对于助教一对一的录音反馈，我会在_____方面进行修改。

A. 语法　　B. 词汇　　C. 作文主题　　D. 标点符号　　E. 篇章结构

（　）5. 对于课堂的集体反馈，我会在_____方面进行修改。

A. 语法　　B. 词汇　　C. 作文主题　　D. 标点符号　　E. 篇章结构

（　）6. 对于反思自评，我会在_____方面进行修改。

A. 语法　　B. 词汇　　C. 作文主题　　D. 标点符号　　E. 篇章结构

三、填充题

请根据在快乐英语写作课上的实际情况，回答下列问题：

1. 我的英文写作提高幅度最大的是_____。

2. 作文多元反馈形式对我的写作提高帮助最大的是_____。

3. 批改网点评让我最受益的方面是_____。

4. 同学互评让我最受益的方面是_____。

5. 助教一对一书面反馈让我最受益的方面是_____。

6. 助教一对一口头录音反馈让我最受益的方面是_____。

7. 课堂集体反馈让我最受益的方面是 _____

_____。

8. 反思自评让我最受益的方面是 _____

_____。

9. 请按照受益程度，将以下几种反馈形式进行排序 _____

_____。

    A. 批改网   B. 同学反馈   C. 助教反馈

    D. 课堂集体反馈   E. 自评反思

四、问答题

16. 在上快乐英语写作课前，你对英语写作反馈的需求是什么？

17. 你在快乐英语写作课上对多元反馈形式最满意的地方是什么？快乐写作课程反馈方式还需要在哪些方面进行改进？

Appendix D-2
Results of questionnaire survey calculated by SPSS

Question No.	Options				
	SD	D	Neutral	A	SA
1	1(4%)	–	3(12%)	11(44%)	10(40%)
2	–	–	1(4%)	3(12%)	21(84%)
3	–	–	1(4%)	3(12%)	20(80%)
4	2(8%)	4(16%)	13(52%)	3(12%)	3(12%)
5	–	–	3(12%)	11(44%)	11(44%)
6	1(4%)	–	–	6(24%)	18(72%)
7	–	–	3(12%)	8(32%)	14(56%)
8	–	–	–	8(32%)	18(72%)
9	–	–	1(4%)	4(16%)	20(80%)
10	–	1(4%)	9(36%)	8(32%)	7(28%)
11	–	–	7(28%)	14(56%)	4(16%)
12	–	2(8%)	9(36%)	8(32%)	6(24%)
13	–	1(4%)	5(20%)	12(48%)	7(28%)
14	–	2(8%)	11(44%)	10(40%)	2(8%)
15	–	3(12%)	4(16%)	14(56%)	4(16%)
16	2(8%)	7(28%)	10(40%)	5(20%)	1(4%)
17	2(8%)	6(24%)	12(48%)	4(16%)	1(4%)
18	–	5(20%)	7(28%)	10(40%)	3(12%)
19	2(8%)	6(24%)	9(36%)	6(24%)	2(8%)
20	–	1(4%)	7(28%)	12(48%)	5(20%)
21	–	2(8%)	11(44%)	9(36%)	3(12%)

(Continued)

Question No.	Options				
	SD	D	Neutral	A	SA
22	–	1(4%)	9(36%)	11(44%)	4(16%)
23	–	6(24%)	12(48%)	6(24%)	1(4%)
24	–	2(8%)	4(16%)	12(48%)	7(28%)
25	1(4%)	2(8%)	9(36%)	10(40%)	3(12%)
26	–	–	3(12%)	10(40%)	12(48%)
27	–	2(8%)	5(20%)	7(28%)	11(44%)
28	–	–	1(4%)	10(40%)	14(56%)
29	–	–	2(8%)	11(44%)	12(48%)
30	–	–	1(4%)	12(48%)	12(48%)
31	–	–	1(4%)	8(32%)	16(64%)
32	1(4%)	1(4%)	4(16%)	8(32%)	11(44%)
33	–	–	5(20%)	12(48%)	8(32%)
34	–	–	3(12%)	12(48%)	10(40%)
35	–	–	1(4%)	12(48%)	12(48%)
36	–	–	3(12%)	11(44%)	11(44%)
37	–	–	9((36%))	7(28%)	9(36%)
38	–	–	8(32%)	9(36%)	8(32%)
39	–	–	2(8%)	6(24%)	17(68%)
40	–	–	–	3(12%)	22(88%)
41	–	–	–	3(12%)	22(88%)
42	–	–	–	3(12%)	22(88%)
43	–	–	–	5(20%)	20(80%)

(Continued)

Question No.	Options				
	SD	D	Neutral	A	SA
44	–	–	1(4%)	6(24%)	18(72%)
45	–	–	–	7(28%)	18(72%)
46	–	–	3(12%)	8(32%)	14(56%)
47	–	–	–	4(16%)	21(84%)
48	–	–	–	4(16%)	21(84%)
49	–	–	–	4(16%)	21(84%)
50	–	–	–	3(12%)	22(88%)
51	–	–	2(8%)	10(40%)	13(52%)
52	–	–	10(40%)	8(32%)	7(28%)
53	–	–	3(12%)	11(44%)	11(44%)
54	–	1(4%)	2(8%)	13(52%)	9(36%)
55	–	–	2(8%)	10(40%)	13(52%)
56		13(52%)	9(36%)	1(4%)	2(8%)
57	1(4%)	–	2(8%)	18(72%)	4(16%)
58		1(4%)	1(4%)	15(60%)	8(32%)
59	–	–	3(12%)	14(56%)	8(32%))
60	–	–	3(12%))	15(60%))	7(28%)

Note: There are only 26 items for Question 3.

Appendix E: Samples of reflective journals

Appendix E-1
A sample of task-specific reflective journal

一、说明：请检查自己的"评议之文"任务完成情况，在你做过的内容上打对号。

批改网	互评		教师反馈		自评	
	同学三级评议互评	评议者填写表格熟悉标准	三级评议反馈	口头录音反馈	自评反思报告	修改终稿
√	√	√	√	√	√	√

二、说明：请根据下列提纲完成汉语的反思报告（注：黑体为提纲内容）

1. 通过课堂，你对"评议之文"有了怎样的认识？
答：要概括所评内容，评议的四部曲是提出命题、表明立场、总结优劣、得出结论。我认为在介绍方面要做到简洁，聚焦要点，同时要融入观点。

2. 在完成作业的过程中，你需要怎样的帮助？你大概用了多少时间写完"评议之文"？在书写过程中，我们前面讲过的几个任务训练对你现在的写作有帮助吗？
答：我需要回顾内容，进一步回忆当时的体会和对所评内容的印象。我大概用了1个小时来完成，主要是还要找一些当时的阅读痕迹和感受。在书写过程中，之前的训练让我这次的写作更流畅，每一次写作训练必然都会是有帮助的。

3. 对于"评议之文"的评价标准，你是否在写作文时有清楚的了解？对你写作文有何影响？
答：我认为基本上是了解的。写作时我基本做到了概括内容，突出观点。由于内容较多，为保证结果较为完整，有些必要的内容我没有进行过度简化，评价标准也基本奠定了写作的思路和全文的走向。

4. 在批改网提交了几次？批改网的分数是否可信？你觉得哪些内容很有帮助？批改网哪些方面还需要改进？

答：由于这次批改的结果比前几次好一些，我大概提交了 2 次或 3 次吧。批改网的分数在一定程度上是可信的，作文中有一些基本的语法错误，但有些错误被认为是中式英语，这并不完全正确。批改网的进一步改进需要用户更多的反馈以及设计者进一步深入地考察。

5. 同学互评是以什么样的方式进行的？三级评议模式？表格评议？表格是做为检查项来用的吗？经过几个任务的磨合，小组之间的同学合作是不是更默契了？同学们的意见是不是更有用了？

答：同学互评既有三级评议，也有表格评议。表格有时内容太多，很多东西我感觉说不太清楚，并不是很确定，所以并没有给别人的文章下定论。在多次任务之后，大家更熟了，合作也更加愉快了，当然也更加默契了。同学的意见中总是有很中肯的，一般都是对方最真实的感受，对我的文章还是有很大帮助的。

6. 你自己在给别人评议时是不是更有信心了？为什么？

答：我读别人的文章是用最真实的感受，可能会有一些不太恰当的地方，但我还是会给出自己的观点。我是有信心的，自己的评议也显得像模像样了。在这个课堂上我不仅可以学英语作文，也学到了如何评议。

7. 助教的评议使你具体在哪些方面有改进？你还希望得到哪些帮助？

答：助教一直都是很认真的，我认为助教做得已经很好了，没有什么特别的需要帮助的地方。

8. 小组评议展示给你最大的启示是什么？

答：小组展示给了全班一个交流的机会，我们可以通过这些展示看到别人的评议，总之是互相学习吧。每组的评议都有自己的特点，我们要融合大家的优点，博采众长，融会贯通。

9. **老师对全班的总体报告、讨论对你的修改有哪些促进？**

答：总结是在写完作文和批改完后的再一次课堂讲解，有助于我们最后的修改，也为修改提出了一些建议，给出了方向。我们可以通过同学们的作文了解自己的不足，同时提升自己的能力。

10. **"评议之文"写作的评议和修改的困难之处和收益之处在哪些方面？概要写作的要领是不是都掌握了？**

答：评议之文的困难主要在于每个人评议的对象是不同的，修改相对比较费力，但是我们可以通过这样的过程学到更多的东西。关于写作要领，在课堂总结和修改环节之后，我认为自己掌握得还是比较好的。

11. **其他还有哪些建议？**

答：暂时还没有。

Appendix E-2

A sample of mid-term reflective journal

到目前为止，半个学期已经过去了，我对这门课程的认识也从最初的"快乐"和"写作"转变为现在的"提高"和"积累"。

最初选这门课时我并没有去咨询其他人，仅仅是在选课时被课程说明打动了：一个学期 8 次写作练习，分组互评，每次的写作体裁不一样。想到我自己的英语写作基础本来就很薄弱，这门课程正好能够提高一下写作水平，至少可以写出一些在格式上比较专业的作文。而且这个课程名为"快乐英语写作"，两周写 1 篇文章，对于这学期课业压力较大的我来说没有太大的负担，非常合适。于是在补退选阶段，我就选择了这门课程。

第一次上这门课时，我便被老师关于作业提交方式的说明弄糊涂了。我们一共要提交两次作业，中间还要进行组内互评修改，同时上传到批改网修改，之后再根据助教的反馈进行修改，然后才形成终稿。这复杂的流程让我觉得这门课程可真是麻烦。但是在两次写作互评之后，我开始意识到这门课程并不仅仅是用大量的写作练习来提高学生的写作水平，而是通过精细的写作，即一篇文章经过多次评议和修改，并且和其他同学的写作文章进行比较和借鉴，来使学生认识到不同的文体应该如何构思，如何去写。总之就是两个字——反馈。吸取从他人那里得来的反馈意见，并将自己的反馈传递回去，从而起到互相促进和互相学习的目的。老师也会在课上对上一周的写作进行讲评和总结。有一节课，老师推荐我们看《李艾幸运背后的秘密》，虽然我们的课程和李艾的成功之路没有一点关系，但是我们的课程理念和她成功的关键有一些相似之处。那就是，李艾在和其他人的交流中获知自己的长处所在，然后善加利用，最后获得成功。快乐英语写作则是通过和他人的交流获知自己的不足，然后加以改进，最后完成一篇好的写作。

现在第 8 周已经过去了，我已经完成了 4 个写作任务。无论是自由写作的随性发挥，还是申请信的诚恳自信，又或是议论文的严谨认真，这 4 篇作文让我对英语写作的内涵有了更加全面的认识。相较于那种体裁单一、枯燥无味的的议论文写作，现在的写作让我切实的感受到了英语写作的快乐所在——多种多样的形式和各式各样的自由发挥。在这八周中，我认识到了与他人交流，向他人学习对于自身的有益之处。如果没有组内互评和反馈建议，也许一周写 2 篇文章也不见得会有提高，而且还会增加作业负担。现在，通过两周 1 篇的写作任务，通过和小组成员的合作和交流，我看到了自己的收获与提高。

通过这八周的写作课程，我对自己的评价是：总得来说，除了第 1 次由于补退选的问题，文章写得比较仓促，我应该是很认真地完成了每一篇写作、互评和修改。虽然我没有上交同学的三级评议（以前我一直以为这个是不用交的），但我都很好的把这些评议保存了起来。每次，我都会认真地阅读和分析同学给我的三级评议，从中找到更深层次的问题并加以改进。虽然我的英语写作基础很差，导致我写的每篇文章的初稿都让人难以入眼，终稿也是勉强及格。但是，我都会用我最大的努力对待每一篇文章。虽然我的文章算不上优秀,我的写作水平提高得也不够快,但我认真地做了。如果让我给自己打分的话,虽然达不到 90 分的优秀,但是 89 分我认为还是可以得到的。

Appendix E-3

A sample of end-of-course reflective journal

看着课程作业上一个个的"提交作业"和"查看批阅",我心里有种特别的滋味。

当初,全寝室的同学一起"迷信"学长学姐的话,一窝蜂地选了"快乐英语写作"课程。一开始我本想着轻轻松松地学点东西,修上英语的两个学分。如今,看着我电脑的"快乐英语写作"文件夹里大大小小的 word 文档少说也有 20 个,初稿挨着终稿,评议挨着录音,还有下载的资源,回想这一学期某个周五或周六的下午,听着隔壁寝室传来的新闻系同学的笑声,闻着楼道时不时飘过的奶茶香、泡面味,而我们寝室里或是三四个同学一起或是独自一人守着电脑,不时查个词典,不时百度一下……好不容易把作文写完了,再感受下互评的打击,哎,一把辛酸泪……

嘿嘿,戏说几句。先抑后扬嘛。

坦白说,这门课确实不"水",贯穿整学期的每两周一次的写作训练,我收获了许多。写完初稿——提交批改网——小组互评——教师评议——上课集体评议——听评议录音——接着修改,走完这一套完整的写作流程,怎么会没有收获呢!除了英语写作水平这方面的收获,其实在与人相处方面,我收获得更多。在选这门课程之前,我也上过一些英语写作课,虽然也有分组,但同学们仅仅是在某一周的某几天联系一下,完成写作任务后就再也不联系了。但是在"快乐英语写作"小组,我们不仅互评作文,还会聊着彼此的学习和生活。每周如果有一个人完成了写作,其他人就得抓紧了。这就像是形成了一个良性循环的圈子,每个人都在用心的学习,且正是这份用心起到了互相督促的作用。很别致,不是吗?我会珍惜这份同学情谊的。

　　我之前很少会找老师或是助教答疑,更别说聊天了。记得有一次要找老师签字,老师都不知道我的名字。这学期,我不仅加了老师的 QQ,居然还看了老师的全家福。另外,在这学期,我第一次收到录音形式的作业批改,第一次添加了助教的微信,并成了好友,第一次收到助教在社交平台上的评论,第一次收到了来自日本的礼物,第一次去研究生公寓,第一次领奖的奖品是苹果和橘子……很显然,这和以往我习惯的和助教相处的模式完全不同,却特别精彩。这门课就像是打开了一扇心窗,让我们看到了彼此的世界。

　　我不知道别人眼中的"快乐英语写作"是什么样的,课业重不重,快不快乐。我是觉得真的很快乐,并且感动。一门课程让人快乐也许很容易,但能让人感动或是感激就很不容易了,"快乐英语写作"课程做到了。

Afterwords

This book seeks to contribute to feedback research by putting forward an integrated feedback approach, placing the development of student agency at the core of the feedback process involved for one task. There has been very little research on how students actually engage with feedback from different feedback sources in succession for one task and how this kind of feedback strategy shapes their writing process, revising practices, and their self-evaluation capacities. The results of this study can help language teaching practitioners and researchers to better understand how the integrated feedback approach could impact EFL writing learning and teaching, and suggest ways to incorporate this approach into writing programs. Specifically, the study is significant in the following aspects.

First, this book contributes to the promotion of a process-oriented approach to writing in the College English writing learning and teaching context in China. Keh (1990) has pointed out that feedback is a crucial element in implementing a process-oriented approach to writing. In the tertiary EFL writing learning context in Mainland China, the process-oriented approach is much needed but it is difficult to use due to objective obstacles such as limited time and big classes (Wang, 2008). Moreover, the lack of an effective and operationalized feedback scheme might be another factor. This current research is trying to add a new push in this direction to help teachers promote a process-oriented writing approach in a more interactive and productive way as the integrated feedback approach suggests.

Second, researchers have stressed the need for more studies which consider the effects of feedback within the total context of teaching (Ferris, 1997; Ferris et al., 1997; Hyland, 2010; Hyland & Hyland, 2006; Prior, 1991). However, contextual factors in feedback studies receive little attention in the literature (Ellis, 2010), as Goldstein (2001) commented that "the research has been largely non-contextual and non-social" (77). This study not only investigates feedback processes but also emphasizes the function of effective instructional supports which was rarely discussed with the feedback engagement in other research. Hence, incorporating contextual factors as an important part of the classroom reality into the study is one step forward in the area of feedback research.

Third, there is a need for more studies which investigate students' perspective on feedback and the factors which influence their feedback engagement, both with the feedback they receive from their instructors (Hyland, 2010) and other sources such as a peer, a computer and himself or herself. In addition to considering students' writing performance, this research explores more of the impact of the integrated feedback approach on students' perceptions of EFL writing learning. Once these perceptions are understood, it may be possible to develop effective feedback techniques to improve students' writing that maintain the perceived positives and limit the perceived negatives.

Fourth, this study can provide insights into how to lead students to be confident writers. It is always important to keep in mind that learners are people who have agency and "actively engage in constructing the terms and conditions of their learning" (Lantolf & Pavlenko, 2001: 45). Storch & Wigglesworth's 2010 study provides evidence that learners do develop an affective response to the type of written corrections they receive, which influences how they process it. Thus, the potential of feedback will only be realized if learners are willing and motivated to engage with it.

This study is written from a Chinese College English writing teaching practitioner and an English writing assessment researcher's perspective. As a College English writing teacher for more than 15 years, the author is quite familiar with students' frustration and instructors' helplessness in the learning and teaching of writing skills in College English classes. As an English writing assessment researcher, the author is trying to explore a new feedback scheme to facilitate students' learning to write in the EFL tertiary context and its impact on students' learning process. The teacher-researcher perspective of this study can bring a practical point of view to the study without necessarily transferring findings from previous research that was conducted in dissimilar contexts, or in laboratory-like conditions

(Lee & Coniam, 2013).

Although this research resulted in some preliminary findings of the impact of an integrated feedback approach in improving students' writing performance, it is, however, an exploratory study and has several limitations.

First, limitations have been identified in the research design in two aspects. The first one is that there was not a control group. However, the variables of the control group are very hard to control, thus, the idea of using a control group was rejected. Moreover, it is a study with an exploratory nature and does have enough data to address the research focus. The second problem is that students' perceptions should be measured by a pre-course questionnaire to form a comparison with the end-of-course questionnaire. In addition, the views only represented those of a sample of Chinese students in this particular research context. The extent to which they may represent students in other contexts is debatable.

Second, limitations have been identified in data gathering and the interpretation of the results. The researcher should have analyzed the feedback and revision first, and then interviewed the writers regarding their revisions and the changes they made. By doing this, the clarification between the use of teacher feedback and self-correction would be clearer.

A final limitation is the difficulty of attributing effects to any single factor. This study shows how a combination of contextual and pedagogical factors interact holistically within the integrated feedback approach, but how individual factors contribute specifically to the implementation of the integrated feedback approach needs further investigation. The students most likely received input from the classroom lecture and feedback workshop or outside of the writing course. Of course, the mere act of rewriting leads most writers to make changes without feedback from themselves, which is very hard to detect and research.

Despite these limitations mentioned above, the findings and conclusions drawn from this research not only expand the empirical data available, they are also suggestive of a number of further avenues to be pursued in future research.

Data analysis in Chapter 4 and Chapter 5 pointed to the existence of individual differences in the way the participating Chinese EFL tertiary learners processed and made use of feedback from different feedback processes in their writing. As Hyland 2010 advocated, more longitudinal qualitative studies which focus on how individual students experience, understand, interpret and engage with feedback in a naturalistic setting are needed, tracing their development over a period of time. In order to know more about individual needs, growth of the student-writers, and their use of feedback from different sources, case studies of individual learners from different groups engaging with the integrated feedback over a period of time will be a topic worth exploring in the future to provide a more nuanced and complex picture (Bruton, 2009; Sachs & Polio, 2007) of the potential of the hybrid feedback system to bring about language improvement.

Students all voted the combination of teacher's written and recorded oral feedback as the most effective link of the feedback system. However, the research on oral feedback in writing is quite limited in the literature (Hyland & Hyland, 2006), and the effects of oral response on revision and longer-term writing improvement have not been fully investigated. Specifically, how the individualized feedback is given as a combination of written and oral feedback has not yet been extensively explored. More studies are required to further evaluate students' perceptions of recorded oral feedback, how they might best be prepared to make the most of them and the effects of the combination of recorded oral feedback, not just on immediate revisions, but on the longer-term development of students as writers.

In the writing classroom, students' voices need to be heard to help instructors plan their feedback strategies (Lee, 2007). There is a need for more studies which investigate the students' perspective on the integrated feedback approach with thinking protocols to understand the nuances of the students' engagement of different feedback information from different feedback sources to explore how the different stages of the integrated feedback coordinate and collaborate to improve students' writing thoroughly.

The practical constraints of real-life contexts are often not considered when recommending feedback practices (Hyland, 2010). Although the instructional support for the course was partially explored in the study, in future studies, more qualitative researches are needed to investigate the role played by contextual factors influencing students' use of feedback.

In addition to the various possible lines of research mentioned above, this research would argue that the most important item for future research agenda would be the investigation of the long-term effects of the integrated feedback approach on learning of writing. This is an issue of crucial theoretical relevance in SLA research, and of the upmost pedagogical importance in instructed SLA, particularly in EFL contexts, given the prominent role that the printed word plays in these contexts and the writing-to-learn purposes that generally characterize the teaching of writing in these settings.

Despite these limitations mentioned above, this study contributes to the literature in proposing a four-stage integrated feedback approach in the framework of AFL. To conclude, the integrated feedback approach has a positive impact on students' perceptions of learning how to write as well as their writing performance; it promotes a community learning classroom culture as well as strengthens students' confidence as L2 writers. While the current study has attempted to answer the research questions posed earlier, it has also brought out issues and research directions that need to be further explored in the future. In doing so, it provides insights into both what teachers may do as they design their feedback procedures with different feedback processes integrated to respond to student work and what students may have gained if they are trained in this approach in their English writing learning.

In the future, teacher feedback may still have an important part to play, but placing too much credence in its powers of influence can lead to students' over-dependence on teachers' feedback only. As a result of attempts to overcome the limitations of teacher feedback, internationally, there is an emerging recognition of benefits associated with the use of alternative methodologies that shift a proportion of the responsibility for assessment to the students in higher education. A far-reaching conclusion, and one that the research has gradually drawn as it has proceeded, is that rather than focusing so much attention on providing feedback and seeing this as a central part of our identifies as writing teachers, with help of the educational technology, we should perhaps devote more attention to developing students' ability to provide feedback among themselves and to themselves.

Bibliography

Amores, M. 1997. A new perspective on peer editing. *Foreign Language Annual, 30* (4), 513-523.

Anson, C. M. 1997. In our own voices: Using recorded commentary to respond to writing. *New Directions for Teaching and Learning, 69*, 105-113.

Askew, S. & Lodge, C. 2000. Gifts, ping-pong and loops—linking feedback and learning. In S. Askew (Ed.), *Feedback for learning*. London: Routledge, 1-17.

Assessment Reform Group. 2002. *Assessment for learning: 10 principles*. Cambridge: Cambridge University Press.

Barley, R. & Garner, M. 2010. Is the feedback in higer education assessment work the paper it is written on? Teachers' reflections on their practices. *Teaching in Higher Education, 15* (2), 187-198.

Beach, R. &. Eaton, S. 1984. Factors influencing self-assessing and revising by college freshmen. In R. Beach & L. Bridwell (Eds.), *New directions in composition research*. New York: Guilford Press, 149-170.

Beason, L. 1993. Feedback and revision in writing across the curriculum classes. *Research in the Teaching of English, 27* (4), 395-421.

Bereiter, C. 2003. Foreword. In S. Mark, & B. Jill (Eds.), *Automated essay scoring: A cross disciplinary approach*. Mahwah: Lawrence Erlbaum Associates, vii-ix.

Bereiter, C. & Scardamalia, M. 1987. *The psychology of written composition*. Mahwah: Lawrence Erlbaum Associates.

Berg, C. 1999. The effects of trained peer responses on ESL students' revision types and writing quality. *Journal of Second Language Writing, 8* (3), 215-241.

Black, P. , Harrison, C. , Lee, C. , Marshall, B. & William, D. 2003. *Assessment for learning: Putting it into practice*. Berkshire: Open University Press.

Black, P. , Harrison, C. , Lee, C. , Marshall, B. & William, D. 2004. Working inside the Black Box: Assessment for learning in the classroom

(Cover story). *Phi Delta Kappan, 86* (1), 9-21.

Black, P. , McCormick, R. , James, M. & Pedder, D. 2006. Assessment for learning and learning how to learn: A theoretical inquiry. *Research Papers in Education, 21* (2), 119-132.

Black, P. & William, D. 1998. Inside the Black Box: Raising standards through classroom assessment. *Phi Delta Kappan, 80* (2), 139-148.

Black, P. & William, D. 2003. In praise of educational research: Formative assessment. *British Educational Research Journal, 29* (5), 623-638.

Black, P. , & William, D. (2009). Developing the theory of formative assessment. *Educational Assessment, Evaluation and Accountability, 21* (3), 5-31.

Blackmore, S. 1999. *The meme machine.* London: Oxford University Press.

Bos, W. & Tarnai, C. 1999. Content analysis in empirical social research. *International Journal of Educational Research, 31*(8), 659-671.

Boud, D. 1986. *Implementing student self-assessment.* London: Routledge.

Boud, D. 1988. *Developing student autonomy in learning.* London: Routledge.

Boud, D. 1995. *Enhancing learning through self-assessment.* London: Routledge.

Boud, D. , Cohen, R. & Sampson, J. 1999. Peer learning and assessment. *Assessment and Evaluation in Higher Education, 24* (4), 413-426.

Brinko, T. 1993. The practice of giving feedback to improve teaching, what is effective? *The Journal of Higher Education, 64* (5), 574-593.

Brock, N. 1990. Can the computer tutor? An analysis of a disk-based text analyzer. *System, 18* (3), 351-359.

Brooks, N. 1961. Language and language learning. *Hispania, 44* (1): 194.

Bruffee, K. 1984. Collaborative learning and the "conversation of mankind". *College English, 46* (7), 635-652.

Burstein, J. & Marcu. D. 2003. Developing technology for automated evaluation of discourse structure in student essays. In M. Shermis & J. Burstein (Eds.), *Automated essay scoring: A cross-disciplinary perspective.* Mahwah: Lawrence Erlbaum Associates 209-230.

Burstein, C. , Chodorow, M. & Leachock, C. 2004. Automated essay evaluation: The Criterion online writing service. *AI Magazine, 25* (3),

27–36.

Butler, L. & Winne, H. 1995. Feedback and self-regulated learning: A theoretical synthesis. *Review of Educational Research, 65* (3), 245–281.

Carless, D. 2006. Different perceptions in the feedback process. *Studies in Higher Education, 31* (2), 219–233.

Carless, D. 2011. From testing to productive student learning: Implementation of assessment for learning. *Assessment in Education, 12* (1), 39–54.

Carless, D. , Joughin, G. & Liu, M. 2006. *How assessment supports learning: Learning-oriented assessment in action.* Hong Kong: Hong Kong University Press.

Carless, D. , Salter, D. , Yang, M. & Lam, J. 2010. Developing sustainable feedback practices. *Studies in Higher Education, 30* (5), 1–13.

Carson, G. 2001. Second language writing and second language acquisition. In T. Silva & K. Matsuda (Eds.), *On second language writing.* Mahwah: Lawren Erlbaum Associates, 191–199.

Carson, G. & Nelson, L. 1994. Writing groups: Cross-cultural issues. *Journal of Second Language Writing, 3* (1), 17–30.

Caulk, N. 1994. Comparing teacher and student responses to written work. *TESOL, 28* (1), 181–187.

Chapelle, C. 2001. *Computer applications in second language acquisition: Foundations for teaching, testing, and research.* Cambridge: Cambridge University Press.

Chapelle, A. & Douglas, D. 2006. *Assessing language through computer technology.* Cambridge: Cambridge University Press.

Chaudron, C. 1984. The effects of feedback on students' composition revisions. *RELC Journal, 15* (2), 1–15.

Chen. C. & Cheng, W. 2008. Beyond the design of automated writing evaluation: Pedagogical practices and perceived learning effectiveness in EFL writing classes. *Language Learning and Technology, 12* (2), 94–112.

Cheng, W. & Warren, M. 1996. Hong Kong students' composition revisions in English language courses. *Asian Journal of English Language Teaching, 6,* 61–75.

Coniam, D. 2009. Experimenting with a computer essay-scoring program based on ESL student writing scripts. *ReCALL, 21* (2), 259–279.

Connors, J. & Lunsford, A. 1993. Teachers' rhetorical comments on student papers. *College Composition and Communication, 44* (2), 200–223.

Cotterall, S. & Cohen, R. 2003. Scaffolding for second language writers: Producing an academic essay. *ELT Journal, 57* (2), 158–166.

Crooks, J. 1988. The impact of classroom evaluation practices on students. *Review of Educational Research, 58* (4), 438–481.

Cumming, A. & So, S. 1996. Tutoring second language text revision: Does the approach to instruction or the language of communication make a difference? *Journal of Second Language Writing, 5* (3), 197–226.

Curtis, A. 2002. Hong Kong student teachers' responses to peer group process writing. *Asian Journal of English Language Teaching, 11*, 129–143.

Dawkins, R. 1976. *The selfish genes.* London: Oxford University Press.

Dikli, S. 2006. An overview of automated scoring of essays. *Journal of Technology, Learning, and Assessment, 5* (1), 1–36.

Ellis, R. 2010. The theoretical framework of investigating written and oral corrective feedback. *Studies in Second Language Acquisition, 32* (2), 335–349.

Elliot, S. & Mikulas, C. 2004, April 7–11. *The impact of MY Access! use on student writing performance: A technology overview and four studies.* American Educational Research Association Annual Meeting, San Diego, United States.

Faigley, L. & Witt, S. 1981. Analyzing revision. *College Composition and Communication, 31* (4), 400–414.

Falchikov, N. 1986. Product comparisons and process benefits of collaborative peer and self-assessments. *Assessment and Evaluation in Higher Education, 11* (1), 146–166.

Ferris, R. 1995. Student reactions to teacher response in multiple-draft composition classrooms. *TESOL Quarterly, 29* (1), 33–53.

Ferris, R. 1997. The influence of teacher commentary on student revision. *TESOL Quarterly, 32* (2), 315–339.

Ferris, R. , Pezon, S. , Tade, R. & Tinti, S. 1997. Teacher commentary on student writing: Descriptions and implications. *Journal of Second Language Writing, 6* (2), 155–182.

Ferris, R. 1999. The case for grammar correction in L2 writing classes: A response to Truscott, *Journal of Second Language Writing*, 8 (1), 1–11.

Ferris, R. 2003. *Response to student writing: Implications for second language students.* Mahwah: Lawrence Erlbaum Associates.

Ferris, R. 2004. The "grammar correction" debate in L2 writing: Where are we, and where do we go from here? (and what do we do in the meantime...?). *Journal of Second Language Writing*, 13 (1), 49–62.

Freeman, S. & Sperling, M. 1985. Written language conference. In S. W. Freeman (Ed.), *The acquisition of written knowledge: Response and revision.* Norwood: Ablex, 106–130.

Fries, C. 1945. *Teaching and learning English as a foreign language.* Ann Arbor: Univerisity of Michigan Press.

Goodfellow, J. 1998. Constructing a narrative. In J. Higgs (Ed.), Writing qualitative research. Sydney: Hampden Press, 175–187.

Goldstein, L. 2001. For Kyla: What does the research say about responding to ESL students. In T. Silva & P. Matsuda (Eds.), *On second language writing.* Mahwah: Lawrance Erlbaum Association, 73–90.

Grant, L. & Ginther, A. 2000. Using computer-tagged linguistic features to describe L2 writing differences. *Journal of Second Language Writing*, 9 (2), 123–145.

Grimes, D. & Warschauer, M. 2006, April 7–11. *Automated essay scoring in the classroom.* American Educational Research Association Annual Meeting, San Diego, United states.

Guo, Q. 2012. *The use of an automated writing evaluation program from EFL learners' perspective.* Master's thesis. University of Chinese Academy of Sciences.

Hall, C. 1990. Managing the complexity of revising across languages. *TESOL Quarterly*, 24 (1), 43–60.

Hall, K. & Burke, W. 2003. *Making formative assessment work: Effective practice in the primary classroom.* Berkshire: Open University Press.

Halbach, A. 2000. Finding out about students' learning strategies by looking at their diaries: A case study. *System*, 28 (1), 85–96.

Hamp-Lyons, L. & Heasley, B. 1987. *Study writing.* Cambridge: Cambridge University Press.

Hamp-Lyons, L. 2001. Fourth generation writing assessment. In T. Silva & K. Matsuda (Eds.), *On Second Language Writing*. Mahwah: Lawrence Erlbaum Associates, 117–125.

Hamp-Lyons, L. 2003. Writing teachers as assessor of writing. In B. Kroll, (Ed.), *Exploring the dynamics of second language writing*. Cambridge: Cambridge University Press, 162–190.

Hamp-Lyons, L. 2007. The impact of testing practices on teaching: Ideologies and alternatives. In J. Cummins & C. Davison (Eds.), *International handbook of English language teaching*. Norwell: Springer, 487–504.

Hayes, R. 1996. A new framework for understanding cognition and affect in writing. In M. Levy & S. Ransdell (Eds.), *The science of writing*. Mahwah: Lawrence Erlbaum Associates, 1–27.

Hayes, R. & Flower, J. 1983. Uncovering cognitive processes in writing: An introduction to protocol analysis. In P. Mosenthal, L. Tamor, & A. Walmsley (Eds.), *Research on writing: Principles and methods*. New York: Longman, 206–219.

Hattie, A. 1987. Identifying the salient facets of a model of student learning: A synthesis and meta-analysis. *International Journal of Educational Research*, 11 (2), 187–212.

Hattie, J. & Timperley, H. 2007. The power of feedback. *Review of Educational Research*, 77 (1), 81–112.

Hawe, E. , Dixon, H. & Watson, E. 2008. Oral feedback in the context of written language. *Australian Journal of Language and Literacy*, 31(1), 43–58.

Hedgcock, J. & Leflowitz, N. 1994. Feedback on feedback: Assessing learner receptivity to teacher response in L2 composing. *Journal of Second Language Writing*, 3(2), 141–163.

Herrington, A. & Moran, C. 2001. What happens when machines read our students' writing? *College English*, 63(4), 480–499.

Hirvela, A. 1999. Collaborative writing instruction and communities of readers and writers. *TESOL Quarterly*, 8(2), 7–12.

Holmes, J. 1988. Doubt and certainty in ESL textbooks. *Applied Linguistics*, 9(1), 20–44.

Hyland, F. 1998. The impact of teacher written feedback on individual writers. *Journal of Second Language Writing, 7* (3), 255–286.

Hyland, F. 2000. ESL writers and feedback: Giving more autonomy to students. *Journal of Language Teaching Research, 4* (1), 33–54.

Hyland, F. 2003. Focusing on form: Student engagement with teacher feedback. *System, 31* (2), 217–230.

Hyland, F. 2010. Future directions in feedback on second language writing: Overview and research agenda. *International Journal of English Studies, 10* (2), 171–182.

Hyland, F. & Hyland, K. 2001. Sugaring the pill: Praise and criticism in written feedback. *Journal of Second Language Writing, 10* (3), 185–212.

Hyland, K. & Hyland, F. 2006. State of the art review on "Feedback in second language students' writing". *Language Teaching, 39* (2), 83–101.

Jacobs, L. Zingraf, A. Wormuth, R. , Hartfiel, F. & Hughey, B. 1981. *Testing ESL Composition: A Practical Approach*. Rowley, MA: Newbury House Publishers.

Jarvis, S. , Grant, L. , Bikowskia, D. & Ferris, D. 2003. Exploring multiple profiles of highly rated learner compositions. *Journal of Second Language Writing, 12* (4), 377–403.

Joughin, G. 2008. *Assessment, learning and judgement in higher education*. London: Springer.

Jones, S. & Tanner, H. 2006. *Assessment: A practical guide for secondary teachers* (2nd ed.). London: Continuum.

Keh, L. 1990. Feedback in the writing process: A model and methods for implementation. *ELT Journal, 44* (4), 294–304.

Krashen, S. 1984. *Writing: Research, theory and applications*. Oxford: Pergamon Institute of English.

Lantolf, J. & Pavlenko, A. 2001. Second language activity theory: Understanding second language learners as people. In M. P. Breen (Ed.), *Learner Contributions to Language Learning: New Directions in Research*. London: Longman, 141–158.

Laufer, B. & Nation, P. 1995. Vocabulary size and use: Lexical richness in L2 written production. *Applied Linguistics, 16* (3), 307–322.

Lave, J. & Wenger, E. 1991. *Situated learning: Legitimate peripheral participation*. Cambridge: Cambridge University Press.

Leki, I. 2006. Coaching from the margins: Issues in written response. In B. Kroll (Ed.), *Second Language Writing*. Cambridge: Cambridge University Press, 57–68.

Lee, I. 2004. Error correction in L2 secondary writing classrooms: The case of Hong Kong. *Journal of Second Language Writing, 13* (4), 285–312.

Lee, I. 2007. Feedback in Hong Kong secondary writing classrooms: Assessment for learning or assessment of learning? *Assessing Writing, 12* (3), 180–198.

Lee, I. & Coniam, D. 2013. Introducing assessment for learning for EFL writing in an assessment of learning examination-driven system in Hong Kong. *Journal of Second Language Writing, 22* (1), 34–50.

Liu, J. 1997 March 11–15. *A comparative study of ESL students' pre-/post-conceptualization of peer review in L2 composition*. The 31st annual TESOL convention, Orlando, United States.

Liu, J. & Hansen, J. 2002. *Peer response in second language writing classrooms*. Ann Arbor: University of Michigan Press.

Lo, J. & Hyland, F. 2007. Assessment for learning: Integrating assessment, teaching, and learning in the ESL/EFL writing classroom. *The Canadian Modern Language Review, 64* (1), 199–213.

Lockhart, C. & Ng, P. 1995. Analyzing talk in peer response groups: Stances, functions and content. *Language Learning, 45* (4), 605–625.

Long, M. & Porter, P. 1985. Group work, interlanguage talk, and second language acquisition. *TESOL Quarterly, 19* (2), 305–325.

Lundstrom, K. & Baker, W. 2009. To give is better than to receive: The benefits of peer review to the reviewers' own writing. *Journal of Second Language Writing, 18* (1), 30–43.

McGroarty, M. & Zhu, W. 1997. Triangualation in classroom research: A study of peer revision. *Language Learning, 47* (1), 1–43.

Mendoca, C. & Johnson, K. 1994. Peer review negotiations: Revision activities in ESL writing instruction. *TESOL Quarterly, 28* (4), 745–768.

Merriam, B. 1988. *Case-study research in education*. San Francisco: Jossey-Bass.

Miao, Y. , Badger, R. & Leder, N. 2006. A comparative study of peer and teacher feedback in a Chinese EFL writing class. *Journal of Second*

Language Writing, 15 (3), 179–200.

Milton, J. 1997. Providing computerized self-access opportunities for the development of writing skills. In P. Benson & P. Voller (Eds.), *Autonomy and independence in language learning.* London: Longman, 237–263.

Mittan, R. 1989. The peer review process: Harnessing students' communicative power. In D. Johnson, & D. Roen (Eds.), *Richness in writing: Empowering ESL students.* New York: Longman, 207–219.

Nelson, G. & Carson, J. 1998. ESL students' perceptions of effectiveness in peer response groups. *Journal of Second Language Writing, 7* (1), 113–131.

Nelson, G. & Murphy, J. 1992. An L2 writing group: Task and social dimensions. *Journal of Second Language Writing, 1* (3), 171–193.

Nelson, G. & Murphy, J. 1993. Peer response groups: Do L2 writers use peer comments in revising their drafts? *TESOL Quarterly, 27* (1), 135–141.

Nicol, J. & Macfarlane-Dick, D. 2006. Formative assessment and self-regulated learning: A model and seven principles of good feedback practice. *Studies in Higher Education, 31* (2), 199–218.

Norris, J. & Ortega, L. 2006. The value and practice of research synthesis for language learning and teaching. In M. Norris & L. Ortega (Eds.), *Synthesizing research on language learning and teaching.* Philadelphia: John Benjamins, 3–50.

Oleksak, R. 2007. Building a framework for national assessment literacy. *Foreign Language Annal, 40* (4), 565.

Orrell, J. 2006. Feedback on learning achievements: Rhetoric and reality. *Teaching in Higher Education, 11* (4), 441–456.

Patton, Q. 1990. *Qualitative evaluation and research methods.* London: Sage Publications.

Peck, W. 1990. The effects of prompts on revision: A glimpse of the gap between planning and performance. In L. Flower, V. Stein, J. Ackerman, M. Kantz, K. McCormick & W. Peck (Eds.), *Reading to writing: Exploring a cognitive and social process.* New York: Oxford University Press, 156–169.

Pennington, C. & Brock, N. 1990. Process and product approaches to computer-assisted composition. In C. Pennington & V. Stevens (Eds.), *Computers in applied linguistics*. Clevedon: Multilingual Matters, 79–109.

Prior, P. 1991. Contextualizing writing and response in a graduate seminar. *Written Communication, 8* (3), 267–310.

Ramaprasad, A. 1983. On the definition of feedback. *Behavioural Science, 28* (1), 4–13.

Raimes, A. 1991. Errors: Windows into the mind. *College ESL, 1* (2), 55–64.

Riordan, T. & Loacker. G. 2009. Collaborative and systemic assessment of student learning: From principles to practice. In G. Joughin (Ed.), *Assessment, learning and judgement in higher education*. Dordrecht: Springer, 175–192.

Rollinson, P. 2005. Using peer feedback in the ESL writing class. *ELT Journal, 59* (1), 23–30.

Sadler, R. 1989. Formative assessment and the design of instructional systems. *Instructional Science, 18* (2), 145–165.

Sadler, D. R. 1998. Formative assessment: Revising the territory. *Assessment in Education, 5* (1), 77–85.

Sachs, R. & Polio, C. 2007. Learners' uses of written feedback on an L2 writing revision task. *Studies in Second Language Acquisition, 29* (1), 67–100.

Sengupta, S. 1998. Peer evaluation: "I am not a teacher". *ELT Journal, 52* (1), 19–28.

Shermis, D. , Burstein, C. & Bliss, L. 2004. April 28–30. *The impact of automated essay scoring on high stakes writing assessments*. National Council on Measurement in Education, Annual Meeting, San Diego, United states.

Shepard, A. 2005. Linking formative assessment to scaffolding. *Educational Leadership, 63* (3), 66–70.

Sommers, N. 1982. Responding to student writing. *College Composition and Communication, 33* (2), 148–156.

Stoddard, B. & MacArthur, C. 1993. A peer editor strategy: Guiding learning disabled students in response and revision. *Research in the Teaching of English, 27* (1), 76–103.

Storch, N. & Wigglesworth, G. 2010. Learners' processing, uptake, and retention of corrective feedback on writing. *Studies in Second Language Acquisition, 32* (2), 303–304.

Taylor, P. 1981. Content and written form: A two-way street. *TESOL Quarterly, 15* (1), 5–13.

Tara, M. 2001. The use of tutor feedback and student self-assessment in summative assessment tasks: Towards transparency for students and for tutors. *Assessment and Evaluation in Higher Education, 26* (6), 606–614.

Tara, M. 2005. Assessment—summative and formative—some theoretical reflections. *British Journal of Educational Studies, 53* (4), 466–478.

Torrance, H. & Pryor, J. 1998. *Investigating formative assessment: Teaching, learning and assessment in the classroom.* Buckingham: Open University Press.

Torrance, H. & Pryor, J. 2001. Developing formative assessment: Using action research to explore and modify theory. *British Educational Research Journal, 27* (5), 615–631.

Tsui, A. & Ng, M. 2000. Do secondary L2 writers benefit from peer comments? *Journal of Second Language Writing, 9* (2), 147–170.

Tsui, A. 2004. The impact of e-feedback on the revisions of L2 writers in an academic writing course. *Computers and Composition, 21* (2), 217–235.

Tunstall, P. & Gipps, C. 1996. Teacher feedback to young children in formative assessment: A typology. *British Educational Research Journal, 22* (4), 389–404.

Truscott, J. 1996. The case against grammar correction in L2 writing classes. *Language Learning, 46* (2), 327–369.

Truscott, J. 1999. The case for "against grammar correction in L2 writing class": A response to Ferris. *Journal of Second Language Writing, 8* (2), 111–122.

Vygotsky, L. S. 1978. *Mind in society: The development of higher psychological process.* Cambridge: Harvard University Press.

Wang, N. 2008. *A study of the efficiency of feedback on students' writing in English.* Doctoral dissertation. Tsinghua University.

Ware, P. 2005. Automated writing evaluation as a pedagogical tool for writing assessment. In A. Pandian, G. Chakravarthy, P. Kell & S. Kaur

(Eds.), *Strategies and practices for improving learning and literacy*. Selangor: Universiti Putra Malaysia Press, 174–184.

Warschauer, M. & Ware, P. 2006. Automated writing evaluation: Defining the classroom research agenda. *Language Teaching Research*, 10 (2), 157–180.

Webb, M. & Jones, J. 2009. Exploring tensions in developing assessment for learning. *Assessment in Education: Principles, Policy & Practice*, 16 (2), 165–184.

Weir, J. 1990. *Communicative language testing*. New York: Prentice-Hall.

Wenger, E. 1998. *Communities of Practice: Learning, Meaning, and Identity*. Cambridge: Cambridge University Press.

Wiggins, G. 1993. *Assessing student performance*. San Francisco: Jossey-Bass.

William, D. 2001. An overview of the relationship between assessment and the curriculum. In D. Scoot (Ed.), *Curriculum and assessment*. New York: Ablex Publishing, 165–181.

William, D. & Thompson, M. 2007. Integrating assessment with instruction: What will take to make it work? In A. Dwyer (Ed.), *The future of assessment: Shaping teaching and learning*. Mahwah: Lawrence Erlbaum Associates, 53–82.

Xu, Y. & Liu, Y. 2009. Teacher assessment knowledge and practice: A narrative inquiry of a Chinese college EFL teacher's experience. *TESOL Quarterly*, 43(3), 49–513.

Yang, D. 2004. Using *MyAccess* in EFL writing. *Proceedings of 2004 International Conference and Workshop on TEFL & Applied Linguistics*. Taipei: Ming Chuan University.

Yang, L. 1995. Trends in the teaching of writing. *Language Learning Journal*, 12(2), 71–74.

Yorke, M. 2003. Formative assessment in higher education: Moves towards theory and enhancement of pedagogic practice. *Higher Education*, 45 (4), 477–501.

Zamel, V. 1985. Responding to student writing. *TESOL Quarterly*, 19 (1), 79–101.

Zellermayer, M. 1989. The study of teachers' written feedback to students' writing: Changes in theoretical considerations and the expansion of research contexts. *Instructional Science, 18* (2), 145–165.

Zhang, S. 1995. Re-examining the affective advantages of peer feedback in the ESL writing class. *Journal of Second Language Writing, 4*(3), 209–222.